The Art of
RUBBER STAMPING

Easy as 1-2-3!

By Michele Abel

CREATIVE PRESS
MINNETONKA, MN

ISBN 0-9630756-2-4
Library of Congress Catalog Card Number: 91-90590

Cover and text design by MacLean & Tuminelly

Text illustrations by Lisa Wagner

Product photography by Paul Lundquist Photography except gift wrap photo—courtesy of *RubberStampMadness* Magazine

Printed by Palmer Printing, St. Cloud, Minnesota

Inquiries and orders should be addressed to
Creative Press
3000 St. Albans Mill Road
Minnetonka, Minnesota 55343

Publishers Distribution Service
121 East Front Street, Suite 203
Traverse City, MI 49684

Acknowledgments

Thanks for all the time and help from Pat Niemuth and family; Donna Gellman, the "Bag Lady"; Gary Dorothy, Stampa Barbara; Dee Gruenig, Posh Impressions; Rosemary McLain Ware, Rosemary McLain Ware Artworks; Russell Bloch, A Classical Pair; Jackie Levanthal, Louise Burns, Pat Samarin and all my friends at Hero Arts.

A special thanks to my family: to my kids, Stefanie and Howard Friedman; and especially to my husband, Michael.

Table of
CONTENTS

INTRODUCTION 1

PROLOGUE 3

LET'S GET STARTED 5
- Basic Supplies 5
- Care Of Your Stamps 11
- Storage 13

THE 3 EASY STEPS 17
- #1—Stamp 18
- #2—Color 22
- #3—Sparkle 26

TRICKS AND TECHNIQUES............31

- Your Imagination......................32
- Supplies..............................38
- Embossing............................39
- Masking..............................46
- Repetition...........................50
- Stampinguides™.......................53
- Stamp Positioner™ 56
- Reverse Images 60
- Die-Cuts 63
- 3-d Cards 68
- Pop-Out Cards 70
- Pop-Up Cards 73
- Stencils 78
- Water Color 81
- Sponging.............................88

ABC's OF STAMPING 95

- ● Add-Ons................................98
- ● Advent Calendar 99
- ● Bank Checks..........................101
- ● Book Covers 101
- ● Bookmarks 102
- ● Bookplates...........................102
- ● Books 103
- ● Borders..............................105
- ● Boxes 106
- ● Calendars 107
- ● Camp Stationery 110
- ● Children's' Parties..................111
- ● Comic Strips 115
- ● Correspondence.......................116
- ● Coupon Books 116
- ● Easter Eggs 117
- ● Envelopes 118
- ● Envelope Liners......................121
- ● Fabric Stamping......................123

- Flyers...125
- Gift Wrap..125
- Greeting Cards...................................131
- Invitations..134
- Jewelry...137
- In The Kitchen 140
- Labels 141
- Lunch Bags.......................................142
- Magnets 143
- Mail Art 144
- Mat Boards 146
- Name Tags 147
- Newsletters 148
- Notepads..149
- In The Office....................................150
- Paper 150
- Parties..152
- Personal Stationery...........................154
- Photo Albums And Scrapbooks 157
- Photo Greeting Cards........................158

- Picture Frames......................159
- Placecards............................160
- Postcards.............................161
- Puzzles................................162
- Ribbons...............................162
- Rubber Stamp Party...............164
- Stickers...............................166
- Tattoos................................169
- Teacher's Gifts......................169
- Teachers..............................170
- Tennis Shoes 173
- Tranquilizers........................174
- Traveling.............................175
- Valentine Mailboxes...............175
- Window Cards.......................176
- Wood Objects........................179
- Window Cards.......................176
- Wood Objects........................179
- Glossary...............................182
- Resources 184
- Index..................................187

Introduction

Rubber stamps are no longer just a kid's activity for a rainy afternoon. Stamping has developed into a sophisticated art form for adults. Rubber stamps are wonderful gifts, great artist's tools, charming toys, and are obsessively sought-after as collectibles. It's the perfect activity for the busy lifestyle—as a quick, inexpensive and enjoyable way to personalize communications in beautiful and memorable fashion. The rest of the world is now ready for the creative rubber stamping Californians have been doing for years now.

Since this book was written in 1991, many new and exciting rubber stamping techniques have been explored. Hopefully, there will always be new and different things to try in your art, that is what keeps rubber stamping alive and fun. The basics contained in this book, however, have changed very little. Those changes have been updated in this revised edition. I believe rubber stamping will continue to evolve because it is based on collective creativity!

Some rubber stamp designs have come from previous art work and are especially adapted for rubber stamping. Others are original designs created specially for rubber stamping. Many of the stamp company owners are artists themselves. Most companies employ artists and calligraphers for their original designs. Rubber stamp art must be extremely detailed and cut accurately. A good stamp is one that stamps the entire image perfectly—no skipped lines or blank spaces, no blurring. There are hundreds of designs to choose from, including specific designs for teachers, as well as a variety of holiday stamps.

Essential to rubber stamping are the accessories—using color and sparkle. There are embossing powders, special stationery and papers, glitter and sparkles, tools that let stampers create fabulous and sophisticated designs. The stamping industry is headed toward more and more dazzling art forms.

Prologue

Rubber stamping as a hobby is for everyone. A truly creative person can have a wonderful time combining and creating with multiple stamps, colors, glitters, and accessories. However, stamping is also for those of you who do not think you are creative. You do not need to draw to make beautiful designs. You will be amazed by how using rubber stamps and experimenting with the designs will bring out all your latent creative abilities.

People get hooked when they realize how easy it is to be creative. There is a kind of magic. It's a great hobby for collecting and using. There are many collectors out there who have thousands of stamps. The individual stamps and accessories are relatively low-priced, and you can always add to your collection, little by little—that makes this a hobby that is accessible to everyone.

Rubber stamping appeals to many special groups, as well, and makes jobs or hobbies more fun and creative. For example, stamps for teachers are good for grading, encouraging, and instructing. Rubber stamps are also being used by occupational therapists, and others working with those who have physical or mental disabilities, as well as with the elderly.

Just follow the simple instructions, add your own personal touches and ideas, and your family and friends will marvel at your creativity! The more you experiment with the stamps and accessories, the more creative you will become.

KEY

☞   Tip

☞✶   Remember

➡   Example

💡   Idea

🚫   Warning

✔   Check List

*   Check Resources for information

 WARNING: Rubber stamping is addictive! Unlike unhealthy addictions, however, using stamps produces creativity, and is a great stress reliever.

So let's get started.

(9) The 3-D effect. Alphabet stamps NameBrand Name Stamps ©, 1991; diaper pin, Stamp in the Hand ©, 1991.

(10) Postcard. Opalescent angel hair shred added to packages. Stamps: Posh Impressions ©, 1991; Stampendous ©, 1991; RMW Artworks ©, 1991.

(11) Stamps: Hero Arts ©, 1991; RMW Artworks ©, 1991.

(12) Stamps: Hero Arts ©, 1991; RMW Artworks ©, 1991; Stamp in the Hand ©, 1991.

(13) Placecard using the three steps. Stamp, alphabet set; Hero Arts ©, 1991.

(14) Stamps and design by Dee Gruenig of Posh Presents for Posh Impressions ©, 1991.

(15) Stamp by Hero Arts ©, 1991, using the three steps.

(16) Stamps colored on directly with markers. Flowers Posh Impressions ©, 1991; invitation part of a larger design Hero Arts ©, 1991.

(17) The three steps. Stamps, Hero Arts ©, 1991.

(1) Postcard using the three steps. Stamps: Hero Arts ©, 1991; NameBrand Name Stamps ©, 1991.

(2) All stamps Posh Impressions ©, 1991

(3) Super stamp Hero Arts ©, 1991.

(4) Invitation using the 3 steps. All stamps Hero Arts ©, 1991.

(5) Images glittered, angel hair shred added to packages. Stamps: Stampendous ©, 1991; A Stamp in the Hand ©, 1991; Posh Impressions ©, 1991.

(6) Stamps: Posh Impressions ©, 1991.

(7) Stamps: "Thanks" Hero Arts ©, 1991; all others: RMW Artworks ©, 1991.

(8) All stamps and ghost card Hero Arts ©, 1991.

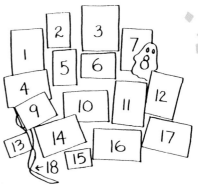

(1) Photo card. Stamps: Posh Impression ©, 1991; A Stamp in the Hand ©, 1991. All die-cut heart cards used in this photo available through Hero Arts ©, 1991.

(2) Window card. Stamp: All Night Media ©, 1991.

(3) Stamps: Hero Arts ©, 1991.

(4) All stamps Hero Arts ©, 1991.

(5) Pop-out card. Flowers colored in with markers on the rubber then glittered, die-cut and glued together. Stamps: Posh Impressions ©, 1991; Stampendous ©, 1991; Stampa Barbara ©, 1991.

(6) 3-D card. Stamps: Posh Impressions ©, 1991; A Stamp in the Hand ©, 1991.

(7) Pop-up card, angel images are 3-D. All stamps Hero Arts ©, 1991.

(8) Stamps: Hero Arts ©, 1991; Raindrops on Roses ©, 1991.

(9) All stamps and card Hero Arts ©, 1991.

(10) Stamp Hero Arts ©, 1991.

(11) Angel card, three basic steps. Stamps Hero Arts ©, 1991.

(12) Bookmark, three basic steps and embossing. Stamps: Hero Arts ©, 1991.

(13) Basket card. Flowers stamped individually on separate glossy paper and cut. A slit made with X-Acto knife above basket top and the flowers were slipped in and taped on back. Stamps: Posh Impressions ©, 1991; Stampendous ©, 1991; Stampa Barbara ©, 1991.

(14) All stamps and die-cut card Hero Arts ©, 1991.

(15) Jewelry designs Dayle Ginsburg. Stamps: Hero Arts ©, 1991.

(1) Greeting card using the three steps. All stamps Hero Arts ©, 1991.

(2) All stamps Stamp in the Hand ©, 1991.

(3) Pop-up card. Basket and eggs stamped separately and put together. Angel hair shred added to the basket. Stamps: Hero Arts ©, 1991; Posh Impressions ©, 1991.

(4), (5), (6) Stamps: Hero Arts ©, 1991; NameBrand Name Stamps ©, 1991; RMW Artworks ©, 1991; A Stamp in the Hand ©, 1991.

(7) Design compliments of Dee Gruenig, Posh Presents, for Posh Impressions ©, 1991.

(8) Stamps: Hero Arts ©, 1991; A Stamp in the Hand ©, 1991.

(9) Stamps: A Stamp in the Hand ©, 1991; Hero Arts ©, 1991; Stampa Barbara ©, 1991.

(10) Stamps: Hero Arts ©, 1991; Stampa Barbara ©, 1991.

(11) The carnation is in 3-D. Stamps: Posh Impressions ©, 1991; Stampendous ©, 1991; Stampa Barbara ©, 1991.

(12) Basket card; flowers done in 3-D, compliments Marilyn Herscleb. Stamps: Stampa Barbara ©, 1991.

(13) Stamps: DeNami ©, 1991.

(14) Stamps: RMW Artworks ©, 1991; Hero Arts ©, 1991.

(15) Stamps: Stampendous ©, 1991; Posh Impressions ©, 1991.

(16) Stamps: Stampendous ©, 1991; Posh Impressions ©, 1991.

(17) Best Wishes stamped on a blue stamp pad, all other images blended directly on the rubber. Stamps: RMW Artworks ©, 1991.

(18) Stamps: Stampa Barbara ©, 1991.

(7) Stamps: Hero Arts ©, 1991; Stampa Barbara ©, 1991.

(8) Stamps: Hero Arts ©, 1991; Posh Impressions ©, 1991.

(9) Stamps: Hero Arts ©, 1991; Stampa Barbara ©, 1991.

(10) Dozen roses stamped using the three basic steps. Stamps: Stampa Barbara ©, 1991; Hero Arts ©, 1991.

(11) Stamps: Hero Arts ©, 1991; Rubber Stamps of America ©, 1991; Stampa Barbara ©, 1991; Posh Impressions ©, 1991.

(12) Earrings stamped in black and embossed with sparkle embossing powder. Stamp Stamp Francisco ©, 1991.

(13) Stamps: Posh Impressions ©, 1991.

(1) Pop-up card. Stamps: Rubber Stamps of America ©, 1991; Posh Impressions ©, 1991.

(2) Stamp: Hero Arts ©, 1991.

(3) Stamps: Hero Arts ©, 1991; Stampa Barbara ©, 1991.

(4) Stamps: Hero Arts ©, 1991.

(5) Stamp: Stampa Barbara ©, 1991.

(6) Stamp: Hero Arts ©, 1991.

All name images used in this photo by NameBrand Name Stamps ©, 1991.

(1) Name stamped and embossed, then cut out. Gold foil origami paper strip glued to glossy card, name glued on top using glue stick.

(2) Stamps: Hero Arts ©, 1991.

(3), (4) Names stamped with colored ink pad and embossed.

(5) Card layered. 3-D. Pansy Hero Arts ©, 1991.

(6) through (9) Names stamped and embossed on vellum stationery.

(10) through (14) Names stamped with colored ink on vellum stationery.

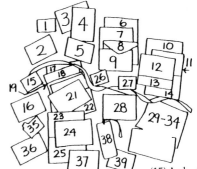

(15) Andy stamped, colored in, and glittered. Die-cut and layered using foil origami paper.

(16) Name is die-cut and glued over foil origami paper under a die-cut heart card.

(17) through (25) All names stamped with a colored ink pad on colored vellum stationery.

(26) Bow stamp Hero Arts ©, 1991.

(27) Name stamped and embossed with sparkle embossing powder.

(28) Name stamped with a rainbow pad and embossed.

(29) through (34) Stationery stamped with rainbow pads on vellum paper.

(35) Die-cut place card. Stamp Posh Impressions ©, 1991.

(36) Card stamped then embossed with silver embossing powder.

(37) All images stamped with rainbow pad and embossed. Design stamps A Stamp in the Hand ©, 1991.

(38) Sponge-like designs stamped with ColorCubes™.

(39) Name embossed with white embossing powder on colored vellum stationery.

(40) Satin ribbon stamped with name and embossed.

All stamps are Posh
Impressions ©, 1991. Gift
wrap and ideas thanks to Dee
Gruenig and staff at Posh
Presents. Photo courtesy
RubberStampMadness
Magazine.

(7) Stamps: Stampendenous ©, 1991; Stampa Barbara ©, 1991.

(8) Birthday card using the three basic steps. All stamps Hero Arts ©, 1991.

(9) through (12) The three basic steps. Stamps: Hero Arts ©, 1991.

(13) Fish card created by blending the marker colors directly on the rubber, stamped on vellum paper. All stamps RMW Artworks ©, 1991.

(14),(15),(16) Flash cards. Stamps: Personal Stamp Exchange ©, 1991; Rubber Stamps of America ©, 1991; Hero Arts ©, 1991.

(17) Satin ribbon stamped with Colorbox™ stamp pads. Stamp: A Stamp in the Hand ©, 1991.

(18) and (21) Stamps: Posh Impressions ©, 1991.

(19),(20) Stamp: RMW Artworks ©, 1991. Accessories: (22), (25) glitter glues, Dazzle™ by Hero Arts ©, 1991; (23) Marvy Markers™; (24) Glue Stick by Zig; (26) Sparkle confetti.

(1) Stamp: A Stamp in the Hand ©, 1991.

(2) Stamps: Posh Impressions ©, 1991.

(3) Create*A*Calendar™ page Creative Impressions ©, 1991. All stamp images using the three basic steps Hero Arts ©, 1991.

(4) All stamps Hero Arts ©, 1991.

(5) Postcard. All stamps Hero Arts ©, 1991. Postcard Creative Impression's Create*A*Postcard ©, 1991.

(6) Stamps Hero Arts ©, 1991.

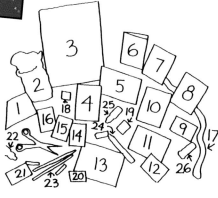

(1) Create*a*Stamp Book™. Creative Impressions ©, 1991.

(2)(3) Sample pages of Stamp Book. Stamps: Hero Arts ©, 1991; Personal Stamp Exchange ©, 1991; Graphistamp ©, 1991; All Night Media ©,1991.

(4) Create*a*Calendar™. Creative Impressions ©,1991.

(5)(6) All stamps: Hero Arts ©, 1991.

(7) Postcard. Stamps: RMW Artworks ©, 1991; Posh Impressions ©, 1991; Raindrops and Roses ©, 1991

(8) Create*a*Postcard™, 1991. Creative Impressions ©, 1991.

(9) Postcard. Stamps: Posh Impressions ©, 1991; Stampendous ©, 1991; RMW Artworks ©, 1991.

(10) Stamps by Hero Arts ©, 1991.

(11),(12) Postcards. Stamps: RMW Artworks ©,1991; NameBrand Name Stamps ©, 1991.

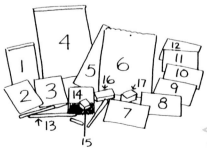

Let's Get Started– The Basics

Rubber stamping is a fun and exciting art. It is limited only by your imagination. Here are some techniques to get you started. But don't stop here. Play around with stamps, combining stamps to get designs, add backgrounds, use a design stamp along with words ("happy birthday", "thank you", "congratulations"). Experiment with colors, glitter, embossing powders. This is the time to let your imagination run wild!

A good thing about rubber stamping is that you do not need to buy everything at once. You can add stamps and supplies as you go along. You can have a wonderful collection of stamps eventually, but to begin with, buy the ones you want to start. This also applies to supplies. You need not start with every colored stamp pad, glitter, embossing powder, etc. As you stamp and experiment, you will discover what new products you want to add, and you can continue to build your collection all the time.

Basic supplies

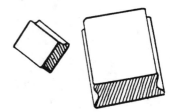

✔Stamp pads

✔ <u>Solid color stamp pads</u> are basic.
Black, blue or dark purple will work best for stamping when you color in the designs.
Other colors are fun for backgrounds, specific designs.

✔ The <u>rainbow stamp pads</u>—both the 3-color and multi-color add a different look to some designs.

☞ To care for your rainbow pads, keep them in the refrigerator when not in use. This will prolong its shelf life.

☞ A certain amount of color blending in rainbow stamp pads is desirable and to be expected. To prevent the colors from becoming muddy, clean your stamp before you use it and between each image if you are doing repetitive stamping.

✔ <u>Colorbox™ stamp pads</u> are another option.

☞ Available in many beautiful colors, these pigment-based colors work well on non-glossy papers.

☞ Use them on all types of papers, glossy and non-glossy, to create impressive techniques with embossing.

☞ They also work well on fabric and wood when embossed.

✓Colored markers

Colored **water-based** markers are used to color in the stamped designs.

☞ Although many brands of **water-based** markers will work, Marvy Markers™ in fine and medium points are preferred for coloring in the designs because they are good clear colors that allow the stamped design to show through. The medium and broad-tipped markers are also wonderful for coloring directly on the rubber.

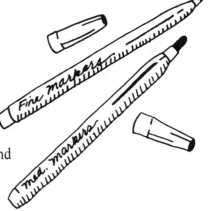

☞ Two other brands of **water-based markers**, LePlume™ and Tombo™, are also great water-based pens to use.

🚫 **WARNING:** Make sure you only use water-based markers when coloring on the rubber, as permanent markers will ruin your stamps.

✓Colored pencils

☞ You can use these to color in the image on <u>non-glossy</u> paper. This will give a completely different look to your stamp designs.

There are also water-color pencils or crayons that are fun to use. After coloring in with these, you brush a small amount of water over the design to get a water-color effect.

✔Glitter glue

This is glue in a small squeezable bottle that has glitter suspended in it. It sells under different brand names. You can get it in many colors as well as clear and iridescent. This adds sparkle to the designs.

✔Prisma* glitter

This also adds sparkle, but it is "chunkier" and gives a more 3-D effect. Prisma* has no adherent of its own, so it is sprinkled over glitter glue, or used with the glue stick. It comes in colors and iridescent.

✔Glue stick

Use this with Prisma* glitter, as well as for many other things. The ideal glue stick has a chiseled end so it can get in small or wide spaces, and it dries quickly.

☞ The glue stick can also be used for embossing with the embossing powder.

☞ Zig* Two-Way Glue Stick™ is the very best to use. It is also sold under the Hero Arts Rubber Stamps, Inc.* name.

✔Embossing powder

Embossing powder gives a raised, sophisticated effect to your projects. Embossing powders are available in many colors, both opaque and transparent. There is also embossing ink that comes in a liquid form to squeeze on a blank stamp pad, and embossing pens.

☞An erasable pen will work for embossing.

✔Paper

Different finishes of paper give different effects to your designs. Paper that is coated and made specially for stamping gives a clear, crisp, professional look to your stamping.

🚫 **WARNING:** There are, however, some glossy paper that are too slick and will not "grab" the ink. Be sure to experiment with the different papers.

✓Stamps

Choose the designs you love, and continue to add designs as you go.

 Use your imagination, don't peg a stamp as only a birthday stamp, or valentine stamp, etc.

Word stamps. Sayings such as "happy birthday", "thank you", "You're Invited", etc. allow you to use your designs in many ways, for different purposes.

 Action stamps. These are designs that can be easily used with other stamps in some way. For example, a bear with an arm up can hold balloons, a flag, flowers, birthday banner.

Taking Care of Your Stamps

Your stamps are practically indestructible and will be yours for a long time. The following section will show you many ways to make your stamps very versatile, and every stamp you collect will be used in many ways.

To keep your stamps in the best possible condition, just follow some simple steps.

Cleaning

It's necessary to clean your stamps between uses if you are changing ink colors (otherwise you will get a muddy look). If you do not change ink colors, clean the stamp whenever you want—each time you are done with each stamp, at the end of your stamping session, or any time in between.

Cleaning your stamps will keep the stamps looking nicer longer. However, if you forget to clean the stamps after each use don't worry. Some stampers only clean their stamps by stamping on a piece of paper until the image is gone.

To clean, you can use a household cleaner, such as ammonia-free Windex* or 409*.

- Spray the cleaner onto a paper towel.

- Blot the stamp on the sprayed towel to remove the ink, then blot on a dry towel. That's all there is to it.

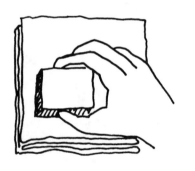 You also may use just a water-dampened towel, or with a little dish detergent and water.

🚫 **WARNING:** DO NOT soak your stamps in water, nor use an oil-base solvent to clean.

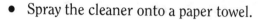

There are also commercial stamp cleaners available. They come in a brush top container.

- Rub the brush over the dirty stamp, then blot on a dry paper towel until clean.

- They are very convenient to use, and they travel easily.

Damp baby wipes also make a great stamp cleaner.

☞ Save the dry wipes to use for drying your stamps off.

Store rubber stamps, rubber side down in a covered box to protect from dirt and dust.

Storage

 WARNING: Store stamps away from heat or direct sunlight. The only way you can ever really damage your stamps is from heat or sunlight, which can harden the rubber, or dissolve the glue backing.

As my stamp collection grows, I have found different ways to store my stamps.

- <u>Plastic tool or tackle boxes</u> with a removable top tray are a great way to start. Line the bottom with a couple layers of stamps, and put stamp pads, pens, glitter, etc. on the top tray.

- Next, I went to <u>plastic shoe boxes</u>, separating the stamps by subject matter—teddies, nature, celebration, Christmas, etc.

- I found a wonderful <u>storage cabinet with plastic drawers</u> big enough to hold 8–10 stamps each, and so I have divided my stamps even further—flowers, backgrounds, wordings, etc. The storage cabinet has 18 drawers, by E-Z Store*. It's sold at discount stores such as K-Mart. There are other similar cabinets with various size and numbers of drawers.

- Another system is the use of <u>stackable cardboard drawers</u>. The drawers can be removed and easily carried to your worktable.

- <u>Elfa Basket Systems</u>* (wire baskets in a frame) also work well. Because of the spacing of the wire grid, you need to store smaller stamps in separate trays so they won't fall through the grid. Or buy the special molded-plastic trays that fit right into the drawers. The 10-frame unit with ten single drawers and the molded plastic inserts is what I have. I put casters on my unit so I could store it out of the way when not in use. I use some of the drawers for my ink pads, pens, glitter, paper supplies and assorted craft accessories.

- If you are lucky enough to have, or find, <u>printer's drawers</u>, these make wonderful storage cabinets. They are narrow enough to lay one layer of stamps flat in the drawer. It's a wonderful way to see what you have.

- For your smaller stamps, you may want to keep them together in little <u>plastic food storage containers</u>, or even those little green plastic strawberry baskets.

☞ Store your older ink pads upside down to bring the ink to the top.

☞ Store rainbow ink pads flat to keep bleeding to a minimum. However, you will find many new, interesting colors as the pad continues to bleed—and that's the beauty of it!

Different stamp companies use different methods for the tops of the rubber stamps. The stamps with laminated tops can be kept clean easily, but those stamps with a raw top, even a lacquered top, will need special care.

💡 To keep them looking good, put clear contact paper or clear packing tape completely over the top and down the sides of the stamps before using them.

The 3 EASY STEPS

The basis of all the techniques and projects in the following chapters are these three steps. After doing demos and running stamping workshops I realized that rubber stamping can be reduced to stamping, coloring, and glittering. This should take the mystery out of how to get beautifully stamped items, but nothing will take the "awe" and "ahh" out of it!

#1–Stamp

Press the stamp on an ink pad, then press on paper.

Hold down a second or two with even pressure. Ink the stamp thoroughly and press firmly. You may repeat a few more times, changing position on the stamp pad. This insures an even wearing of the pad and a good inking of the stamp.

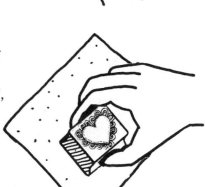

☞ If you are using a rainbow pad with slight separations, tap the stamp up and down a few times along the same color area on the pad to be sure no blank spot will appear where the pad separates.

☞ There is no need to use excessive pressure with the stamp on the pad, nor to pound on it.

☞ After stamping on the pad, hold the stamp at an angle, rubber side towards you. You will then be able to see if the entire surface has been inked. If there are any dry spots, or if the entire rubber does not seem to "glisten", tap on the pad a little more.

Stamp on the paper.

⃠ **WARNING:** Don't wiggle or "rock" the stamp, or the image will be blurred.

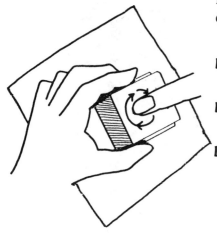

Each stamp has a personality. The size and the distribution of the design on the rubber will often affect how it stamps.

☞ Some stamps may be pressed lightly, others more firmly to get the whole design stamped evenly.

☞ Generally, the larger the stamp, the more pressure will be needed. For smaller images a light touch is fine.

☞ For larger images, hold stamp down firmly with pressure, without rocking the stamp. Hold the stamp with one hand while using your other hand to press evenly over the entire top of the stamp.

☞ Practice with your new stamps. You will soon learn how best to stamp.

An alternative to stamping with an ink pad: Use markers directly on the rubber to color on the stamps.

🚫 **WARNING:** Be sure they are **water-based markers—** permanent ink can damage the rubber on your stamp.

☞ By using markers for color, you do not need to buy every color stamp pad in order to stamp a design in a particular color. If, occasionally, you need a red or orange color to stamp with, you can use your watercolor markers directly on the rubber of your stamps.

➡ For example, to make a couple of greeting cards that you stamped "Merry Christmas" in red, you could use your red marker. However, if you were doing a 100 Christmas cards to mail out, it would be easier to buy a red pad and stamp them.

☞ To see what the stamped design will look like before you stamp on your good paper—you can position uninked stamps on the paper first, to get the best placement; or, use scratch paper to try out different placements.

☞ As a rule of thumb, I usually use at least three stamps to make a good layout:

1. A large stamp—as a focal point

2. A word stamp

3. A small stamp—as a background or accent to tie the designs together

#2–Color In

After stamping on the paper in a solid color, use water-based colored marking pens to color in the image. At this point, it is just like a coloring book.

☞ For most designs, use a basic color stamp pad, such as black, dark blue or dark purple. Once the design is colored in, the color of the outline will make very little difference.

☞ Use markers that are bright, but not opaque. The stamped image should show through the color.

Using Markers on Stamps:

You can use your brush markers directly on the rubber of the stamp to stamp a multi-colored image. By using different colors on different parts of the design, a multi-colored image can be stamped directly on paper.

☞ Use light colors first to avoid getting a darker color on your lighter markers.

🚫 **WARNING:** You must use **water-based markers**.

☞ To moisten the stamp before stamping, breathe on the stamp as you would fog a mirror.

☞ By using markers directly on the rubber of the stamp
you can get a lot of versatility from your stamps.

💡 It is also possible to use only parts of the stamp design
with the use of your brush markers. Using your marking
pen rather than a stamp pad, color directly on the rubber
that part of the design you want to use, then stamp.

☞ What isn't inked won't stamp. This makes your stamps
even more versatile by using the designs in different ways.

➡ For example, you may have a stamp that has a
teddy bear with Happy Birthday and little gift boxes
on it. If you want to use just a gift box, or just the
Happy Birthday, you can do it with markers.

☞ Be sure you are using a clean, dry stamp when you
use this technique.

☞ Stamp pads work well with delicately-lined images, but use colored markers directly on large area stamps. You may use as many colors as you wish on the rubber before stamping it.

☞ After you have colored, breathe on the rubber as if to fog a mirror to put more moisture on the stamp before stamping.

BREATHE!!

#3-Sparkle

Add sparkle to your stamped designs with glitter glue,
Prisma, small sprinkle mylar or opalescent hearts, stars.

- Glitter glue—has the glitter suspended in glue, as well as color.

- Prisma glitter—adds the most brilliant and 3-dimensional look. Prisma has no adherent of its own. It is used with either a glue stick, or for an even more dimensional look, over the glitter glue. It comes in different textures, superfine, fine, and medium. In colors as well as iridescent.

- Sprinkles—mylar and opalescent hearts and stars—used with glitter glue or glue stick to make showers of hearts and stars, borders, much more.

☞ Use clear or iridescent glitter over the stamped and colored images to add sparkle while letting the colors shine through.

☞ Colored glitter glue adds a new dimension. By adding the same color dazzle over the colored image you get a more intense color plus glitter.

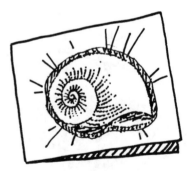

☞ Experiment mixing colored glitter glues over differently-colored designs for fun color changes.

☞ Try gold and silver glitter for some great, unique looks. Use gold or silver on designs stamped with rainbow pads for a beautiful look. Gold and silver adds a sophisticated look to a design.

☞ Just stamp a design in black, then use gold or silver on the black images. This is a great look for Halloween— spider webs, haunted houses, bats, and more!

☞ Use the glue stick to write your name, or draw your own design, then sprinkle on Prisma. Try clear on dark papers, gold or colored glitter on white paper.

💡 Try outlining your designs with a narrow band of glue and sprinkle Prisma* on the glue for a great effect.

💡 The new fluorescent glitter glues are opaque and can be used on their own without color underneath. Try outlining and writing with them, they're wonderful.

☞ To remove Prisma glitter that sticks to the rubber of your stamps, use a piece of cellophane tape.

That's It, Folks!

That's it! Everything you need to know to stamp, and stamp beautifully, has just been told.

- First you **stamped** your stamp on paper with an ink pad or markers. This is the place to create your design by combining stamps.

- Second, you **colored** your designs in.

- Third is the **glitz** step. Use the glitter glue and Prisma to glitter it up.

Now go ahead and start wowing all of your friends with the most beautiful greeting cards and original invitations they've ever seen.

The following section will give you lots of ideas of what you can do with your new-found creative talent. Let your imagination be your guide.

TRICKS AND TECHNIQUES

These "Tricks and Techniques" will give new dimensions to your stamping. You will learn more ways to use the same stamps for new and varied looks.

Let Your Imagination Run Wild!

You now know everything you need to get your rubber stamp design on paper and make it look beautiful. How you use these designs is where your creativity comes in. And for those of you who think you are not creative, you will change your mind just by experimenting with the stamps and varying them.

The looks of your stamped designs depend on a lot of things: how you put the design on paper, what you combine, what you repeat. All of this affects the finished look of the project.

- ☼ Create scenes using stamp designs of clouds, stars, grass, sun, animals, houses, flowers, etc.
- ☼ Add strings to hearts for balloons. Have a teddy hold a bunch of balloons.

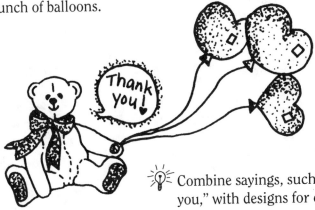

- ☼ Combine sayings, such as "happy birthday" or "thank you," with designs for cards, invitations.

- ☼ Repeat designs to make borders and backgrounds.

 Stamp designs off the edge of the paper for a professional look.

 Hang a spider from a web, or from a cloud, or from "Happy Halloween".

Draw or stamp in grass at the feet of animals or flowers; extend grass to unite multiple designs.

Combine stickers with your stamp images, you will be surprised how many stickers work well with stamps— for example, add a hat sticker on a stamped bear and have him carry a sticker suitcase.

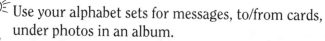

Cut out and glue stamped images on a photo.

Use your alphabet sets for messages, to/from cards, under photos in an album.

Use one large multi-image stamp, such as Hero Arts'* Limited Edition Stamp on the front of a folded notecard and then inside stamp an invitation stamp, happy birthday, thank you, Merry Christmas, etc.

🔅 Use a "Hand Stamped For You" stamp design on the back of your cards and invitations to identify your work. It's your "Hallmark"!

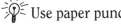 🔅 Use paper punches* available in many sizes and shapes.

- Punch out the little shapes and stamp around the die-punched images, perhaps following a theme— punched hearts on a Valentine, a child's birthday card with teddy bears and punched teddies.

- Punch out the shapes to make a border or a design on the card (punch out on white paper and then back up the card with a colored paper and the punched shapes will really stand out).

- Punch the shapes out of colored paper and glue them onto your stamping project.

🔅 Save the punched shapes and use them as confetti in a card or in invitations.

☞ Small 1/8" hole punches are also wonderful for many craft projects, such as making jewelry. The hole is smaller than a regular hole-punch and gives a very professional, clean look.

The different uses show how versatile each stamp can be, as its look changes by its use. There are many ways to come up with new looks for the particular designs you have, and new ways of working with them. To jog your creativity:

- Stamp out your collection of stamps on individual pieces of paper (use index cards for a good sturdy paper).

- Trim the designs close to the image and store them in a box or envelope.

- When looking for new ideas, sort through these designs, spread them out in front of you, put different design combinations together.

- Stamp out your collection on paper by category: nature, hearts, cats. . . .

- Keep an idea file or notebook handy and jot down new ideas as they come to you.

- Creative Impressions* makes a wonderful notebook of heavy-stock glossy paper in which to keep your ideas, and to keep track of your stamp collection.

- Consider using other techniques and mediums with your stamping:

  ➡ stickers

  ➡ words cut from newspapers or magazines

  ➡ photographs

- When you buy new stamps don't just use it once or twice then toss them in a box; play with them, experiment using them with your other stamps, use different colors to see the different effects you can get.

- Take some classes or workshops to get new ideas.

- Get together with friends—it's amazing to see what different people will do with your designs—they might try some different combinations, or turn them sideways or upside down and get new designs. We often have preconceived ideas of what to do with our stamps, and fail to see, and use, them in totally different ways.

Supplies

Besides your stamps and stamp accessories, you may need these supplies on hand for any of the various projects.

✔ Scissors
✔ X-Acto Craft Knife
✔ Glue Stick
✔ Ruler
✔ Hole Punch

✔ Cellophane Tape
✔ Double-sided foam tape
✔ Scratch paper
✔ Post-It* Notes
✔ Double-sided cellophane tape

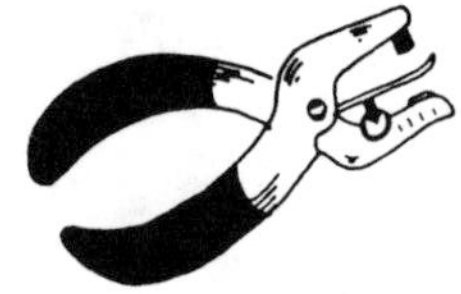

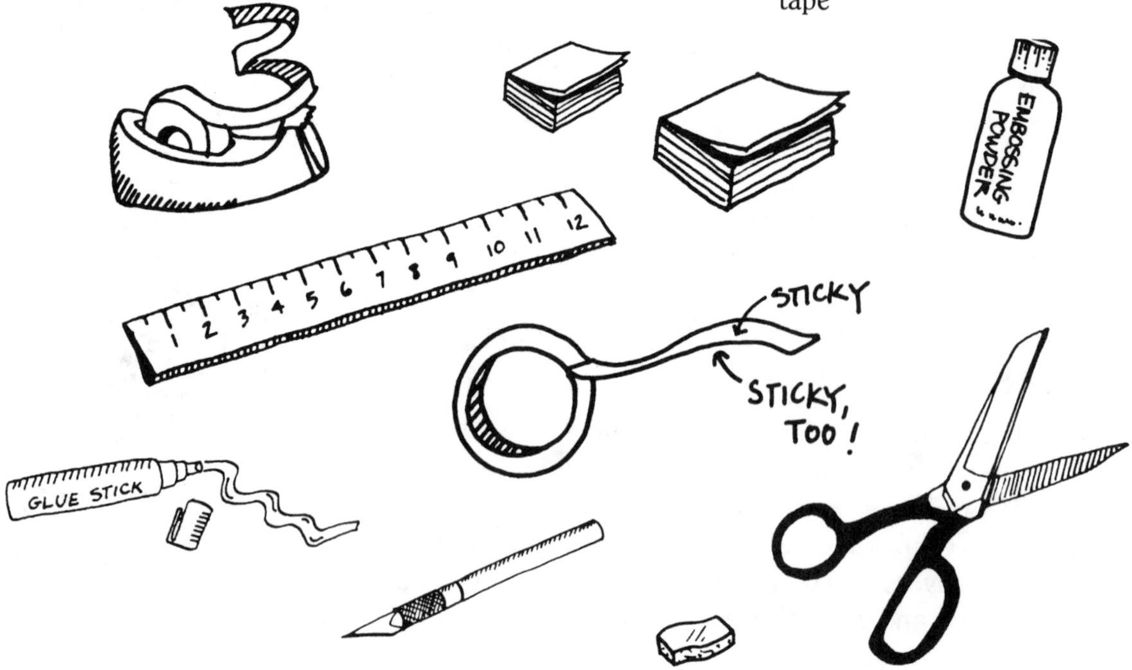

STICKY

STICKY, TOO!

GLUE STICK

EMBOSSING POWDER

Embossing

The technique of embossing is a step between stamping the design and coloring and glittering. To emboss you need a heating element to activate the embossing powder. <u>It should be already heated before you begin.</u>

Embossing powders give a raised, shiny or metallic finish to your stamped designs. Embossing powders come in many colors. Use gold or silver powder over any color ink and the image will be gold or silver. When you use iridescent, pearl, sparkle embossing powder, the color of the ink you use will turn pearly, or glittery.

Types of heat:

- hot plate
- burner on an electric stovetop
- an iron
- over a toaster (good for use with kids)
- an electric light bulb (at least 60 watts)
- in a 300° oven
- heat gun (sold in hobby and craft stores)

With your heat source ready, let's begin:

1. **Stamp your image.** Use good quality paper (glossy paper works great for embossing), using a very wet ink pad, markers, or embossing ink. Embossing ink comes in a liquid that can be applied to a blank stamp pad.

If you use markers on the stamp, be sure to breathe on the rubber, as you would "fog" a mirror, before stamping.

☞ Colorbox™ stamp pads are perfect for embossing because they are very "wet" and hold the embossing powder exceptionally well.

☞ A glue stick can be used to write a name or make a design, then sprinkle the embossing powder on the wet glue.

☞ For writing names and embossing, try a pen with erasable ink—the ink will be wet enough to hold the embossing powder.

2. **Liberally pour embossing powder on the just-stamped image.** Tap it around to cover the entire design, then tap off the excess.

SAVE
THIS

☞ Be very generous with the powder.

☞ Use a paper under your work to save the unused powder and return it to the container.

☞ Use a fine, soft brush to get any excess powder off the paper.

3. Hold the paper a few inches above the heating element. Watch as the embossing powder melts, giving your design a shiny, raised look.

☞ The embossing powder does not always melt evenly, so continue to hold the paper over the heat until the whole design has turned glossy.

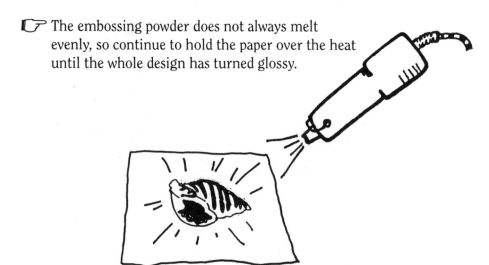

☞ To emboss in the oven:

- Cover the center rack of the oven with a piece of aluminum foil, then preheat the oven to 300 degrees.

- Put the stamped card or cards that have the embossing powder on on the covered oven rack. Do not overlap.

- Push rack into the oven, close the door and remove after two minutes. Make sure the embossing powder has melted. If not, replace in the oven and keep checking.

- Give the embossed image time to set before touching, about 30 seconds.

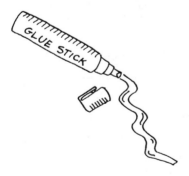

☞ If the cards have bowed during heating, place under a heavy book for about an hour.

☞ Use a glue stick to write or draw on your paper, then use the embossing powder as above.

☼ Try double embossing. Emboss the image with gold or silver. Color the design with markers. Brush embossing ink over the colored-in design. Then sprinkle with a pearl or sparkle embossing powder and emboss the design again. You must use one of the transparent powders to get this stained-glass effect.

With embossing, practice makes perfect. Experiment with
the wetness of the ink you use, the amount of embossing
powder and the right heat. Once you get the hang of it,
embossing is just as simple as stamping.

☞ The principle of embossing is that the powder sticks to
the wet ink of the stamp pad. Therefore, do not let the
ink dry before pouring on the embossing powder. Once
the powder is on the ink you do not need to use a heat
source immediately. You can get a few ready and then
heat them.

🚫 **WARNING:** Oils from your skin can get on the paper
from handling it. If the powder sticks where you don't
want it to stick, blow it away or use a soft brush to brush
it off.

☞ It will take longer for the heat to penetrate on heavy
stock paper; again, you need to experiment.

☞ If the paper you are using is especially dense and you
have trouble embossing, hold the paper upside down
over the heat source. You can even stamp on cardboard,
wood, fabric etc. by turning your work upside down
over the heating element. Or use a heat gun for an easy
way to work with dense material.

☞ Opaque embossing powder such as silver, gold, and solid
  colors cover the ink with its own color. You can use
  these opaque powders to emboss on colored paper—
  such as white ghosts on black paper.

☞ After you have embossed, the finishing is up to you.

  ☼ Leave the embossed design as it is and you have an
    elegant design.

  ☼ Or continue by coloring in with the Marvy
    Markers™ and using glitter.

  ☼ Experiment with the different types of looks you
    can get with a combination of techniques.

Masking

To get the effect of stamped images behind each other, in front of another, coming out of or going into one another, there is a technique called "masking".

1. Stamp the foreground image on your paper (for example, the front animal in a pair or group of animals, the basket to put your flowers in, etc.).

2. Stamp the same image again on a Post-It note.

☞ Stamp close to the top of the paper so that the "sticky" part is on the back of the image.

☞ Or use Dennison's Tack-a-Note*, a temporary adhesive, which can make your scratch paper work like a Post-It note. The glue stick will do the same, if you allow the glue to dry completely before using.

3. Cut out the image carefully, staying <u>inside</u> the outline.

☞ Cutting the mask slightly smaller than the stamped image prevents a gap between the front image and the background. This gap is called a "halo."

4. Place the Post-It note image (the "mask") over the already-stamped image. Now stamp again, overlapping the first. Although you really just stamped the second stamp over the first, it looks as if it is behind.

☞ For a bigger crowd, or more flowers in the basket, etc. continue your masking.

☞ When you stamp a tree or bench or carpet over the
mask, the original figure will appear in front of, against,
or over the new image.

☞ You can use a mask to get a partial image of your stamp
design. Lay a piece of scratch paper on the paper you
are working with. Stamp only the part of the image you
want on your paper, leaving the rest of the image
stamped on the scrap paper.

☞ Use the straight edge of your Post-It note to block
anything with a straight edge in the design such as a
wagon, or a basket. Stamp the images you want to fill
over the straight edge. Again, to prevent a "halo," place
the straight edge just below the top of the image you are
masking. Remove the Post-It and your wagon is filled!

Another type of mask is called a **mortise mask**.

- Stamp an image such as a basket or frame. One that has a large open area.

- Stamp again on scratch paper or a Post-It note and cut out the open area inside the image.

- Now you can stamp flowers, kitties, etc. in the basket; stamp what you want inside the frame, and so on.

🔆 Use this for putting something in a window, or empty TV screen, or fishbowl, etc.

STAMP ON CARD

STAMP AGAIN ON POST-IT AND CUT OUT MIDDLE

CARD WITH IMAGE
POST-IT

🔆 Use envelopes to store your masks. Keep track of where the masks are by stamping the image on the envelope that holds the mask.

Repetition

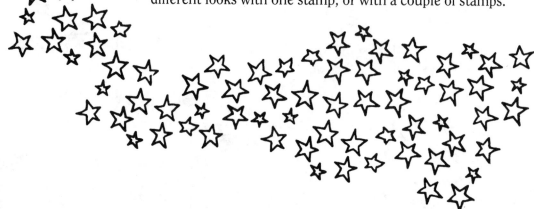

By stamping a design over and over you can get many different looks with one stamp, or with a couple of stamps.

With repetition, one star can become a galaxy; one teddy, animal, etc. can become a crowd, one flower a field of flowers.

One stamp repeated at evenly spaced intervals can make a beautiful border. You can use a couple of designs and repeat every other one to make an interesting border.

One stamp repeated over and over creates an overall pattern and texture. Use a stamp repeatedly with a light color ink pad (such as powder blue, yellow, pink, etc.) to make a background for other stamps, or just to make pretty writing paper out of plain paper. Stamps specially designed for backgrounds are also available.

By turning the stamp a little each time you stamp, you can create the impression of movement. Have a teddy bear tumble down a page, have a leaf fall from above.

☞ Another way to achieve the effect of movement is by "blurring".

- Get a shooting star by stamping the star low. Then, without removing the stamp from the paper, pull the stamp in the direction from which you want it to fall.

- To give a bird flying movement do the same thing: stamp the image, then pull the stamp in the opposite direction of its flight. You will get a fade-out, giving the sense of movement in the direction it's going.

☞ Stamp a number of times without re-inking to give the illusion of depth, the feel of a crowd. The lighter images seem farther away. This gives a textured feel.

🔆 Draw a light pencil circle, then stamp a leaf or leaf border or flower around the circle to make a wreath.

🔆 Use a small stamp, stamped in a geometric shape over and over to achieve unusual effects depending on the designs you use.

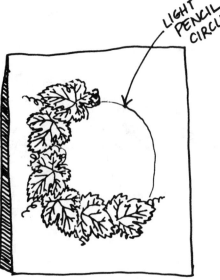

LIGHT PENCIL CIRCLE

StampinGuides™

Stampa Barbara's* StampinGuides™ are a marvelous, innovative graphics tool for stamping beautiful patterns on gift wrap, stationery, fabric. They come in a package of 3 sheets, with six different designs on both sides of the durable plastic sheets. These guides are a wonderful springboard for your imagination. There are endless creative possibilities with the six graphic designs. At 17" x 22", they are large enough to create a large sheet of wrapping paper, but just as easy to use on a gift card.

I have used them to design:

cards	book covers
stationery	invitations
fabric stamping	gift wrap
borders on newsletter and flyers.	

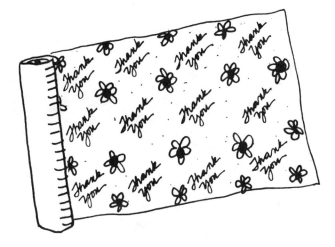

● To use:

1. Unfold the design you want to use.

2. Place it under your paper or fabric. Make sure the paper
or fabric you are using will allow the design on the
StampinGuide to show through.

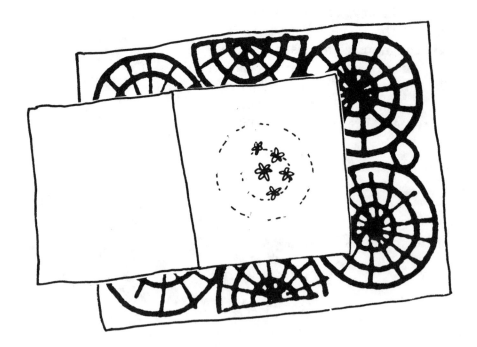

☞ As you stamp, the designs on the guide will bring out your creativity.

☞ The lines and spaces will help you see exciting patterns to make with your stamp images.

☞ You can stamp your designs in bright solid colors or rainbow pads, or color in after stamping.

💡 Add glitter, stickers and other media for more variety.

I put this section under TECHNIQUES because that is what it is. However, it could just as well have gone in the GIFT WRAP section, or BORDERS, BOOK COVERS, STATIONERY; but most appropriately, in the section called TRANQUILIZERS. Once you start to create with these, you will become mesmerized with all the exciting patterns you will get with your stamp images.

Have fun with them, that's what they're for!

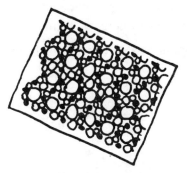

Stamp Positioner™

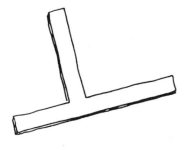

The Stamp Positioner™, brainchild of Stampa Barbara's*
Gary Dorothy, is a wonderful tool to have. Using his See-
Thru Paper™ along with the Stamp Positioner, you can stamp
any image right where you want it. Use the Positioner to
make perfect alignments with your stamps, restamp an image
you "goofed", do your masking to perfection, get double-
image effects, and align borders perfectly.

The basic directions for using the Positioner are:

● To make perfect borders every time:
  ☞ Place the long side of the Positioner along the
     bottom of your paper or where you want the border.
  ☞ Using the Positioner as a guide, stamp along it's
     edge.

● For masking, or restamping a misstamped image:

1. Place the corner of a sheet of See-Thru Paper in a right angle corner of the Stamp Positioner.

2. Mark the See-Thru Paper on the corner and at each end where the paper touches the Positioner. This will help you keep the paper exactly where you want, and keep it from slipping under the Positioner.

3. Stamp your image on the See-Thru Paper by guiding the wooden block of the stamp into the right angle of the Positioner carefully before pressing down to stamp the image.

4. Move the See-Thru Paper image to the spot where you want the image to stamp on your design work.

5. Holding the paper on your card where you want it, place the Positioner so that the See-Thru paper is back again in the right-angle corner as in the first step.

6. Remove the See-Thru Paper and guide your inked stamp into the corner of the Positioner as you did in step 3.

With this technique, you are able to guide your stamp exactly where you want to place it. Although this can be done by "eyeballing," the Positioner gives you an exact placement.

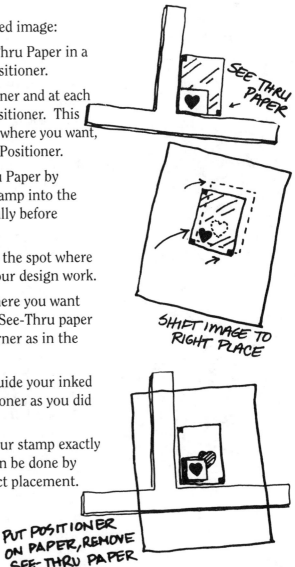

SEE THRU PAPER

SHIFT IMAGE TO RIGHT PLACE

PUT POSITIONER ON PAPER, REMOVE SEE-THRU PAPER AND STAMP

SEE-THRU
PAPER

To use the Positioner to mask perfectly, stamp your front image on your card. (You can use the Positioner for this as well.) Then stamp the image you want behind your design on the See-Thru Paper as in Step 3. Move the See-Thru image around on the stamped design until you like it. With your top image masked, and the See-Thru image where you want to stamp it, follow steps 5 and 6.

➡ For example, use this technique to put teddy peeking thru a train window. Or a person in front, sitting on a chair.

☞ Another use for the Positioner is restamping an image
    that didn't stamp well the first time. Perhaps your
    stamp was too light, or part of the image didn't stamp.

- Stamp the image on the See-Thru Paper.

- Position the See-Thru image exactly over the poorly
  stamped image.

- Carefully place the Positioner with its right-angle on
  the See-Thru Paper.

- Remove the paper, and restamp your design right on
  top of the already stamped design.

By playing with the Positioner, I know you will come up
with lots more ways to use it. Again, let your imagination
guide you.

Reverse Images

Another handy technique is the ability to get reverse images with your stamp designs. When one of your designs faces opposite of what you would like on your particular project, or to make a stamp face one's self—good for borders, for example—you can reverse the design.

1. Use a plain rubber surface, such as a flat-surfaced eraser. There are also stamps made especially for this purpose.

- Ink the stamp design you want to reverse with a stamp pad or markers.

- Work quickly, and breathe on it to keep the ink moist.

- Stamp this image on a plain, large rubber surface (at least as large as the image).

- Stamp the image from the rubber onto your paper.

2. Use cellophane tape:

🚫 **WARNING**: this will only work on <u>glossy paper!</u>

- Stamp a lightly inked stamp design onto the <u>sticky side</u> of the cellophane tape, leaving enough extra room on the tape as a tab to remove the tape after using.

- Wait a few seconds to allow the ink to almost dry on the tape.

- Now press the tape, sticky side with the impression down, on your paper where you want the image.

- Rub the top of the tape a few seconds.

- Slowly, carefully remove the tape from the paper.

☞ If the stamp pad or marker is too wet, the ink will bubble on the tape.

☞ Allow the ink to dry on the tape, otherwise the image will smear when you transfer it from tape to paper.

☞ Use large size packing tape for larger stamps.

🚫 **WARNING:** For non-glossy paper, be sure to use removable tape!

Die-Cuts

With the use of an X-Acto knife, you can cut out all or just part of a stamped (or, stamped and embossed) design to get some unique effects.

● For use with any folded card, especially ones used for placecards or name cards, you can stamp your design over the fold and then cut out the portion on the top half of the fold.

- Lay the card flat.

- Stamp the design so that the portion of the design you want to "peek over" the top is on the upper half of the fold.

- Color and glitter, or emboss first then color.

- Use the X-acto knife and cut out around the image on the upper part of the fold.

- Now fold the card, but not the cut out image, and stand it up.

● Use a Post-it note to block the bottom half of the folded card. Then stamp a design such as a teddy peeking over the top of a card. Again, use your knife to cut out the design above the fold.

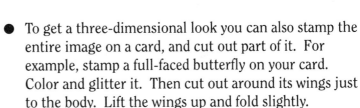

● To get a three-dimensional look you can also stamp the entire image on a card, and cut out part of it. For example, stamp a full-faced butterfly on your card. Color and glitter it. Then cut out around its wings just to the body. Lift the wings up and fold slightly.

● Die-cuts and layering can make some dynamic cards and invitations.

- Making sure the bottom sheet is the size that will fit into your envelope, layer a top sheet that you have die-cut the designs around the edges, and glue onto a bottom sheet, or sheets, of coordinating colors.

- Each succeeding layer should be about 1/4" or more larger than the sheet on top of it.

- Using this technique of layering, stamp the top sheet with a "You're Invited" stamp, or a large "Happy Birthday" stamp. Then layer colored papers behind it. Stamp, color and glitter your designs on a separate sheet of paper, cut them out and lay them over the multiple layers, using the glue stick to hold them in place.

● For a sophisticated look, stamp a design along the bottom and/or sides of a card as a border. Emboss the design for a little extra strength; then, using scissors, cut around the outside edges of the border.

☞ A small curved manicure scissors works great for this.

➡ Stamp a border of large pansies across the bottom of a gift card, then cut out around the bottom of the pansies getting a pretty scalloped affect.

➡ Stamp large hearts around the sides and bottom of a card, cut around the outside edges. Then perhaps, using a glue stick, glue this to a doily for a pretty Valentine or love letter.

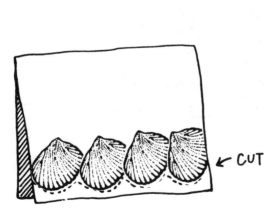

← CUT

3-D Cards and Scenes

Add dimension to your stamping projects. With this technique you can make scenes or just add multi-dimensions.

- Design your card or scene. Stamp it on your paper and color it as you want it.

- Pick out one image or a variety of images you want to "pop-out" at you. Stamp those images on another sheet of heavy paper (the glossy paper is perfect for this). Color these images and glitter them the way you want.

- Using a scissors, cut these designs out.

- Put a small piece of foam-backed double-stick tape on the back of your cut out image and tape it on your card on top of the first image.

- For multi-dimensions, use more layers of tape to vary the heights of the images.

FOAM TAPE

🔅 You could also make a background scene on the card. Then stamp, color and glitter the designs you want in the foreground on another sheet. Cut the designs out. Place these designs where you want them on the scene, using the double-sided tape.

"Pop-Out Cards"

When you open a "pop-out" card, an image is going to "pop out" of the card. The effect will be the same as in those Pop-Up books we had as kids.

● The simplest of this type of card is to use a simple paper "spring".

  ● Using a strip of paper narrower than the image that will jump out, accordion fold the strip.

  ● Use the glue stick and glue one end of the paper to the image (which has been stamped, colored, glittered).

  ● Glue the other end to the inside of the card, placing it where you want it.

AN EXAMPLE OF A POP-OUT CARD WITH A JACOB'S LADDER SPRING

HAPPY BIRTHDAY!

Love, mom + Dad

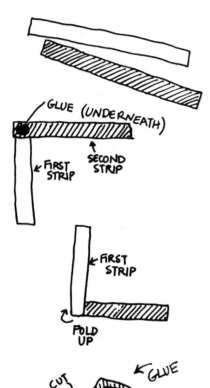

- There is also the "Jacob's Ladder" spring.

  - Cut out two pieces of paper approximately 2 3/4" x 1/4".

  - Put glue on the end of one strip. Lay the other strip at right angles to the first with its edge on the glued part. Allow the glue to dry.

  - Fold the left strip over the right. Bring the strip on the bottom up and over the glued area. Fold the strip on the left side over to the right. Fold the strip on the top down. Continue overlapping until all the paper is folded.

  - Apply glue under the top flap. Bring the flap down and press. Cut off any excess paper.

  - Pull the spring out slightly so it gives.

  - Put glue on the end of the spring and attach it to the back of your stamped design you have cut out.

  - Apply glue at the other end of the spring and attach to the inside of your card from where you want the design to "spring".

Pop-Up Cards

With this technique, when you open the card one or some of
the images inside will "sit up". Just like children's pop-up
books.

✔ You will need two large, or medium-sized, folded cards,
   plus an extra sheet to stamp and cut.

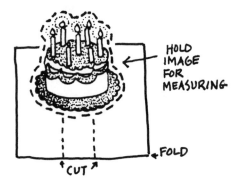

HOLD
IMAGE
FOR
MEASURING

←FOLD

↑CUT↗

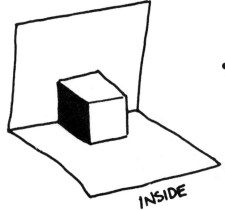

INSIDE

☞ To try this technique, you may want to practice on scrap paper first.

- Stamp the image you want to "pop up" on the extra sheet of glossy paper. Color it and glitter it as you want.

- Cut the image out.

- Take one of the glossy cards and refold it, glossy side inside.

- Take this refolded glossy card and place your cut out image on the top of the card, folded edge of the card at the bottom. Now make two cuts from the folded edge.

  ☞ The width of the cuts should be no wider than the image you are going to mount.

  ☞ The depth of the cuts should be no longer than the distance from the bottom of the fold to the bottom of the cut-out when it is held with its top at the top of the card.

- Open your card and hold it like a tent. Push the strip through to the other side of the card. Close the card and press firmly. Now open and you will see the strip pop up.

☞ Whether you center the strip or put it to one side or another depends on the effect you want.

☞ You can get more depth and create a whole scene by having more than one image pop up on separate strips, some closer to the front of the card for depth.

● Design the rest of the inside with stamps, color and glitter to go along with the pop-up.

☞ Background stamps create a good effect on the top half of the open card, as well as the bottom.

- Decorate the <u>outside</u> of the other glossy card the way you want. Again, color, glitter etc.

- Use the glue stick on the <u>inside</u> bottom half of the <u>inside</u> <u>card</u>. Press it on to the bottom of the open <u>outside card</u>, pressing the inside card up so the folds of the two cards are aligned.

OUTSIDE CARD

INSIDE CARD

- Use the glue stick on the top half of the <u>inside card</u> and press the <u>outside card</u> down so both cards are folded. In this way, your card won't buckle when opened.

- Use the glue stick on the back of the cut-out image and glue it onto the strip.

- You now have a card with a decorated front that opens to a pop-up.

➡ For example, a card that says happy birthday with balloons and confetti on the outside. When opened a stack of presents pop up.

☞ You can also use photos. Take the image from the photo, cut it out and use it like a cut-out stamped image to pop up.

Let your imagination go wild with these cards. They're fun to make, and really not very hard to do.

Using Stencils

With this technique you can create designs within designs.

● Take a piece of post-it paper from which you have cut a design out of the middle of the paper, such as a heart or star, Christmas tree, your initial. The list is endless.

   ● Put this paper over the paper you are going to be using. Make use of the sticky part of the Post-it note to tack down the cut out paper.

   ● Stamp another small design inside the cut-out, overlapping the design over the edge of the cut-out.

   ● Take the top stencil off. You will have your stamped designs in the form of your cut-out.

   ➡ For example, small stars forming the shape of a large star, "I love you" making a heart.

☀ Use the blank space to stamp or write a message, or highlight another stamp image inside.

CUT   REMOVE STENCIL

STENCIL

STAMP

- You can also do this in the reverse.

  - Make a large cut-out on post-it paper, again such as the star or heart. Lay this cut-out over the paper you are using.

  - Stamp all over your paper with whatever image or images you want to use. Over-stamp the cut-out image with the stamped designs so a clear pattern will show when you remove the paper.

  - When you remove your cut-out you will have stamped designs all over your paper except for a blank space in the shape of your cut-out.

Water Color

Give your rubber stamping a water-color look by using brush
and water with your rubber stamped images. This technique
works with rubber stamp images with large rubber surfaces,
as well as delicately lined images.

For stamps with big area images:

Step 1: Blend Your Colors On The Rubber Stamp

- Be sure to use **water-based** markers. The 1500 series of Marvy Markers™ work well for this. Blended color stamp pads may also be used.

- When using markers, put your light colors on your stamp first, going from light to dark to protect the markers.

- Then, go back and blend the lights into the darks. (Blending the darks into the light colors will only cover the light ones.)

  ☞ Because this blending process will cause the lighter markers to lose their purity after awhile, it is a good idea to have two markers of the lighter colors in order to keep one pure.

  ☞ To refresh your marker, you can rub it on a piece of scratch paper to remove the darker colors.

Step 2: Stamp Your Image

- Breathe on your stamp to put moisture on the stamp before stamping.

- Stamp your image.

- You may huff on your stamp, and stamp a few times again without re-inking.

- You might want to mask your first image before restamping. (See MASKING).

Step 3: Use Brush and Water

- Use a small watercolor brush.

- Your brush will pick up the color once it touches your stamped image - you are now painting with color.

- You can fill in every part of the design with the brush, or skip over places as you like.

Step 4: Add Glitter and Other Finishing Touches

Step 1: Stamp Your Images

- Let your images dry long enough that they won't "bleed" when you apply the wet-brush to them.

Step 2: Apply the Wash

- Apply a wet brush over and beyond the images. This is called a "wash".

- Spread the color the brush has picked up.

  ➡ Use this to fill-in the image, or extend the image.

- You can create the illusion of more of the same, or of distance.

  ➡ Extend a few clumps of grass into a lawn.

  ➡ Use the wash over flowers to give the illusion of more flowers behind.

For delicately lined images:

Tips and Techniques

- Stamp a few butterflies on your paper. After the images are dry, wash over them with a wet brush. This will give a hazy look and extend the color. When dry, restamp the images here and there over the dried wash.

- Take the over-stamped image and emboss. This looks really pretty over the delicate wash under it.

- Use an old toothbrush, or large brush, and splatter over the images. Dip in ink or paint and flick to give fine splatter effects.

- For line-image stamps, use water-based stamp pads, markers, or a combination.

☞ Your finished artwork can be waterproofed.

- Spray a fine coat of fixative over your work. Available at most art supply and craft stores.

- Waterproof your work before adding glue and glitter or metallic embossing powder.

• While you are working with your wet paper, the paper may buckle slightly. It will flatten as it dries.

Sponging

You can use sponges to make unusual backgrounds for your stamping projects. Sponges can also be used to create different effects such as feathers, teddy bear fuzz.

✔ Different type sponges for different effects, such as: cosmetic sponges, porous everyday sponges, natural sponges, bath toy sponges, etc.

✔ Cut sponges in small pieces.

✔ Stamp pads in various colors.

You Need:

- Dab the sponge section on the ink, then dab it on your paper using short strokes.

- Use the full width of the sponge for backgrounds on the entire paper.

- Just dab around the edges of the paper for a border effect.

- Put ink just on a flat edge of the sponge to get a feathery look.

- Cut off a small piece of sponge and roll it. Ink it just on the rolled edge to get a "fuzz" effect.

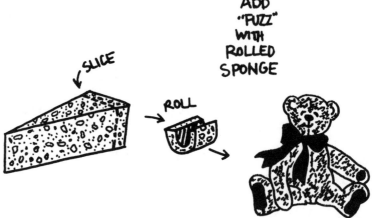

ADD "FUZZ" WITH ROLLED SPONGE

SLICE

ROLL

- Brush the inked sponge across the paper to look like a windy sky. Perfect to fly stamped kites or balloons.

- Lay down ragged cuts of paper or paper towel and tamp a sponge with blue ink over it. Clouds appear!

- Use parts of paper doilies as dainty stencils on your cards for borders or backgrounds. Sponge over the doily to get the designs on your paper.

- Take a paper mask of any shape, such as heart or star, and tamp your inked sponge over it to get that shape on your paper.

- Use a sponge dabbed on pastel ink pads to get beautiful backgrounds.

- Take the edge of the sponge and with blue ink make waves, green ink to make blades of grass.

- Cut your sponge into shapes such as a heart and use to make your own "sponge design".

As you experiment with this technique, you will discover more ideas.

What Can We Do With All of This?

Now do you see how easy it is to use your rubber stamps? There are only three basic steps to stamping. With these three steps you can make beautiful and unusual projects and look like a pro.

You can add any of the techniques to get different effects still using just your three basic steps. You will get a lot of use out of your stamps. Just by combining different stamps or using different techniques, and by adding word stamps, your stamp designs become very versatile and the uses of each stamp is multiplied many times over.

So—what can we do with all of this?

The ABC'S of RUBBER STAMP USE

You've started your collection of rubber stamps. You have all the basic necessities. You've learned the basic steps of stamping. You even know some clever and original techniques for making your stamping really interesting. Your friends are very impressed every time you give them a birthday card. They rave about your creativity and artistic ability.

But there must be more you can do with your new-found talent than making birthday cards and thank you notes!

There is. This section will cover many projects from A to Z. Well, maybe not Z! Hopefully, this will just be the beginning of your creativity. I am sure you will think of more and unique ideas as you play with your stamps.

Add-Ons

When you are making cards and invitations, add other small items along with your stamps to get different looks.

- Add <u>decorative stickers</u>—for example, a hat sticker on a stamped teddy bear, a sun sticker over your stamped flowers, a clown holding sticker balloons.

- Use <u>tiny stick-on bows</u> on stamped packages, or around a very delicate party design.

- Use <u>tiny stick-on ribbon rosettes</u> with your stamped designs.

- Sprinkle <u>mylar confetti</u>, or small mylar shapes on iridescent glitter glue to make confetti around birthday greetings, shooting stars off a "celebrate" stamp.

- Stamp a teddy or a clown on the bottom of the page, add balloons toward the top and connect with <u>curling ribbon</u> or shredded ribbon.

- Use <u>cellophane Easter grass</u> applied with the glue stick for "grass" around flowers.

- Take very finely shredded <u>opalescent mylar angel hair</u> and glue on stamped presents to give the look of half-open boxes.

- Use part of a <u>doily</u> to "wrap" long stemmed roses.

- Go into a craft supply store for more ideas—little <u>googlie eyes</u> for teddy bears, <u>fuzzy balls</u> for rabbits tails, or <u>sequins</u> to glue on.

- Use the sticky side of <u>mailing or address labels</u> to attach all kinds of mylar tinsel and shredded angel hair.

  ➡ For example, cut an opening in a design, such as the top of a gift box. Stick the label to the back of it so that the adhesive side is up—then attach the glittery stuff where you want it.

- Get decorative <u>postage stamps</u> and incorporate them in your designs—for example, a love stamp with a wedding card or a Valentine, a bird stamp, a flag stamp and so on.

Advent Calendar

These calendars are the ones with little windows that open onto a picture or a scene. Open one window for each day from December first to Christmas.

Advent calendars are made with two layers. The top layer contains the main, outside scene and the windows that fold open. The bottom sheet has the images you see when each window is open.

To make this calendar:

- Use heavy paper stock for the top sheet so the underlying designs will not show through.

- Create the scene for the top sheet and decide where the 24 windows will go.

- Stamp and color your scene.

- Cut each window carefully on three sides. Use an X-Acto knife. Number each window.

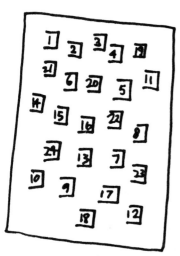

- Now place the bottom sheet under the top and make tiny pin holes on the 4 sides of each window to show where the windows are. Stamp your hidden designs inside each of these marks.

- Color and glitter your images.

☞ Be sure to leave a margin around all four sides of the bottom sheet to have room to glue the two sheets together.

- Glue around the four edges and carefully stick the two sheets together.

SECRET STAMPS
AT EACH "X" SPOT

DECORATE
WITH SCENE

←GLUE
TOGETHER
AT
EDGES

Christmas Spirit

Personalize your bank checks! Stamp a design in the corner of your checks. Or, using a light-colored stamp pad (such as powder blue, pink, peach), stamp a background design, repeating the design. You can stamp over the front of the check wherever you'd like your design as long as the check is still readable.

Bank Checks

🚫 **WARNING:** The back has only a limited amount of space for the endorsement. The rest of the back is reserved for bank use, and your bank has the right not to accept the check if that part is written in or stamped on. So it's best to leave the back undecorated!

BACK

Books

Book Covers

Cover books with plain paper. Use grocery sacks or heavy plain white paper. After making the cover, use your stamps to decorate the cover.

💡 This is also a good way to give a book as a present.

💡 Book covers are ideal for use with StampinGuides™.

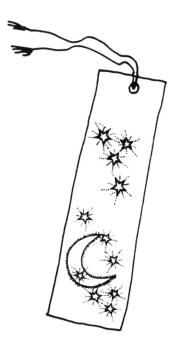

Bookmarks

Use glossy bookmarks you can find at stores that sell rubber stamps and accessories. Or make your own.

-🔆- After decorating your bookmarks you can laminate them if you wish. There are materials available for laminating them yourself or take it to a printer or sign shop. If you are making quite a few, make them on a single sheet of paper. Then laminate the sheet and cut out the individual bookmarks.

-🔆- The prepackaged bookmarks have holes at the top and come with tassels. You can use these as gift cards as well. Make the bookmark, put in the tassel, then attach this to your package by running the ribbon on the package through the hole. Now you have a beautiful, hand-made gift tag that probably won't be thrown away.

Bookplates

Bookplates are great to put in all of your books. When you lend your books, your name will be on a beautifully stamped bookplate inside the book.

-🔆- A set of personalized bookplates would make a beautiful gift.

You can use blank labels to make the bookplates or get glossy "crack and peel" sticker sheets from a printer. Using special stamps that say "this book belongs to..." or, with your alphabet set and your own stamp designs, make up bookplates.

💡 To add special appeal to the bookplates, color and glitter the designs.

💡 Emboss the designs for a sophisticated look.

💡 Use your alphabet set to put the name on all the bookplates.

Books

Make your own book! Make a book as a gift. Make it around a theme—such as age for a birthday, or memories, a special holiday, for a couples anniversary, as a story for a special child—the list could go on and on.

- Stamp each page to make a story, color and glitter it, even make a pop-up book for kids or adults.

- Take the book to a printer. A printer can bind the book with a plastic comb, or pad the book.

- There is a good notebook made of high gloss stamping paper made especially for stamping that would work great for this, made by Creative Impressions*.

You can also make a book made from one sheet of 8 1/2" x 11" paper. Follow the template and directions. You can bind it with a three-hole stitch. Use embroidery floss and needle and follow the instructions.

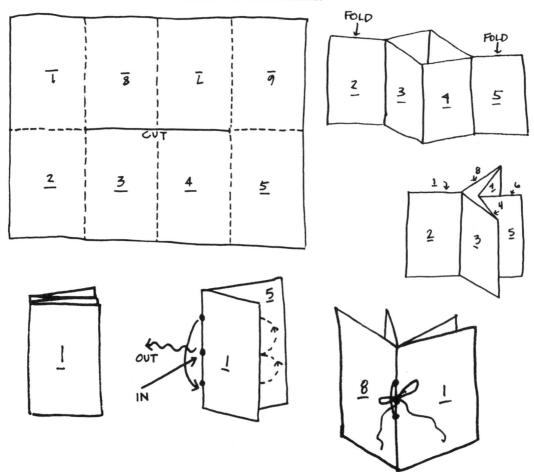

Make a flip book for kids, or better yet, let the kids make these. Flip books are a succession of pictures where a main image appears to move, jump, dive, etc. as you flip through the pages of the book.

Borders are easy to make. Simply use one design or a couple of stamp designs. Stamp the designs side by side across the bottom and/or top of your paper, or on all four sides. Another look is to alternate a couple of designs along the border.

Borders

There are stamps that are designed as borders. There are also stamp designs in the form of a "frame". These designs go around the four sides and usually are the size to fit a gift enclosure card.

Stamps on rollers also make great borders. It takes some practice to get the rollers to roll straight, but it is an easy way to make borders and design gift wrap once you get the feel of it.

Boxes

Take plain boxes and cover with paper stamped with designs you've colored and glittered.

- ⌾ You can make boxes with lids for holding trinkets.
- ⌾ Make a box and lid for holding stationery you've designed and have the box match the stationery.
- ⌾ Cover just the bottom of a box to hold decorated memo paper.

🚫 **WARNING:** If you use glossy wrap paper in either white or a color, check to make sure the paper is stampable. With white or light colors you can stamp and color your design right on the paper. If you would like to use a dark paper, use glossy white sticker paper to stamp the designs on, then cut around the image leaving a white border and stick on the box.

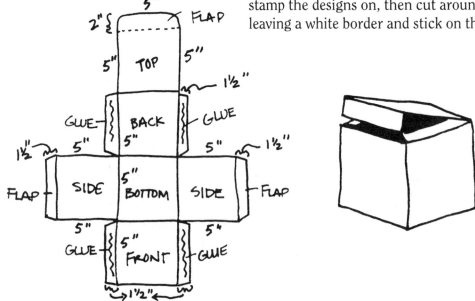

How To:

- Measure and cut the paper to a size that will cover the box (two separate pieces, one for the bottom, one for the lid) and will fold over into the inside.

- You can now stamp, color and glitter the paper.

  ☞ Keep in mind what part of the paper will be showing—mainly the sides of both sections, and the top of the lid.

- Place the box on the wrapping paper. At the four side corners, snip out a wedge of the paper even with the edge of the box to make a mitered edge. Fold the end flaps up and glue them inside, then fold over the sides and glue them down.

What a wonderful way to say I love you all year long! Make your own calendar or use a calendar made for rubber stamping, such as CREATE•A•CALENDAR* by Creative Impressions*. Use alphabet sets and number sets to stamp in the month and days. Since you are creating your own calendar, you can start at any month of the year.

Calendars

Fill in with appropriate images for birthdays, holidays, special events. This is a wonderful format to use all your stamps in a timely fashion.

Ideal for making a special gift, personalized for the person you're gifting.

Your best friend. Stamp out all the dates that are meaningful to you and your friend. A good birthday gift, get well gift, Christmas gift. A perfect anniversary gift for your favorite couple.

☼ <u>Mother, Dad, Grandparents</u>. A great Mother's or Father's Day gift or Christmas or birthday gift.

☼ <u>Teacher</u>. As a gift from one student, or the whole class can make one together. It also makes great Scout and Sunday School projects.

☼ <u>Baby gift</u> for new parents. Since your calendar can start with any month, any year, start this one on the day of baby's birth and end on baby's first birthday! Mark all the special first holidays, and even relatives birthdays, and let Mom and Dad mark in all the special firsts. What a wonderful keepsake!

☼ The <u>child leaving the nest</u>. Put in all the holidays, relative's birthdays (perhaps with a reminder to send a card or call), put "I love you" and "call home" interspersed among the messages.

☼ A <u>family history calendar</u>. Use the calendar for months with no specific year, and make a calendar highlighting important events in your family history, and all the birthdays, anniversaries, special occasions relating to your specific family.

Camp Stationery

Make stationery to send along to camp with a camper. The best bet for keeping those letters coming is to make postcards!

- Decorate the front side of the postcards with your stamps and color and glitter it up.

- You may want to decorate it with memories of home, or what they will be doing at camp.

- You might even make writing easier by giving them items to check off—I am having a (great, wonderful or marvelous) time; I miss you (a little, a lot, who are you?); the kids here are (great, fun, dorky).

- Self-address the postcards and stamp them.

- Enclose a cute pen, and it makes a great going away gift.

- This would also be a good way to hear from college students away at school.

- This is also a good going away gift for a friend, or a bon voyage gift for friends going on a long journey.

Childrens' Parties

Getting a group of children together with stamps and a project is a natural. And it is a wonderful way to keep them busy. The age of the kids and their abilities will determine how long and how much supervision will be needed. Preplan the party so there will be little or no surprises along the way.

- Consider the space you have and the personality of the group to determine how many children you can handle.

  ☞ I have found that 6 to 10 children is just about perfect.

  ☞ The age group can be anywhere from perhaps 7 to teenagers.

  ☞ If the party is bigger than 10, consider enlisting another adult to help you.

- Pick a project that will fit the theme of the party, if there is a specific one. Parties such as birthdays, Halloween, Valentine's Day lend themselves perfectly, but any theme will be great.

☞ Be sure that the table you are going to use is covered with a plastic tablecloth or butcher paper.

- Have all the stamps laid out where it will be easy for everyone to either reach or pass around.

  💡 Putting the stamps on a washable plastic tray or trays is ideal.

  💡 Put marking pens in plastic glasses.

- Make sure you have enough stamp pads, markers, glitter glue.

- Projects you can have the kids do:

  - birthday hats
  - bookmarks
  - party bags
  - Halloween trick-or-treat bags
  - Valentine cards

To follow your theme, see the section on parties for ideas on making invitations and other party goods with your stamps. Now that you have the party planned, the date picked, the theme in mind, you need an agenda:

First 5 minutes: Get everyone in their places. Explain a little about rubber stamps and the way they are used. Show them the ink pads, markers, etc. so th⟩ will know what they will need to make their project.

<u>15 minutes:</u> Give a mini demo. Show them the three basic steps to making a stamped project. Depending on their ages, you may want to go into some simple techniques such as masking, repeating, even die-cuts (be sure to have scissors). Most importantly, teach them how to clean the stamps after each use. Show them that clean stamps are more fun because the colors are clear, not muddy. Give them all damp paper towels or even easier, have baby wipes for them to use. The rule is: each stamp must be cleaned after its use.

<u>30–45 minutes:</u> Give them paper to practice with and whatever materials they will need to make the project. Have plenty of extra paper for those who work faster than others.

<u>Last 5–10 minutes:</u> When they are finished with their projects: Have them all make sure the stamps are cleaned, the tops are back on the markers and glue, the stamp pads are closed. If it's possible, they can put everything away as well. Generally, the kids will have fun with this part too.

Here are some party-theme and project ideas:

➡ Birthdays—party hats, bookmarks

➡ Valentine's—cards and envelopes, Valentine mailboxes

➡ Easter—Easter eggs, Easter egg-shaped cards

➡ Halloween—trick or treat bags, pumpkin-shaped cards, haunted house cards or scenes

➡ Thanksgiving—placecards, napkin rings

➡ Christmas—cards, calendars, tree ornaments, gift wrap

➡ Hanukkah—gift wrap, banners

➡ New Year's—party hats, invitations

➡ Mother's and Father's Day—calendars, picture frames or picture cards

➡ Summer party—t-shirts, tennis shoes, visors, camp stationery

You will be surprised how a group of kids of any age can get engrossed in something so fast. With just a little pre-planning on your part, a stamping party can be a very easy way to entertain kids.

Comic Strips

You can make your own comic strips using rubber stamps. Create an idea of what you want to do. The strip can be one box, or a strip of any number of boxes.

- Draw your boxes on paper, keeping in mind the size of box needed for the size or sizes of your images.

- Stamp the designs inside the boxes.

- You can add dialogue using a dialogue or thought balloon, or stamp the description on the bottom of each box.

- Use your comic strips to make greeting cards, get well cards, a unique invitation design, a cover for a notepad, etc.

Correspondence

Accent your correspondence with a variety of rubber stamp designs.

Make designs on borders, or use the images to illustrate or highlight part of your correspondence. Experiment with different types of paper for different effects on your correspondence and the stamped designs.

💡 Use a design or a stamped scene as your logo or your letterhead, or as part of your signature!

Coupon Books

Stamp out a coupon book for mother, father, sweetheart, children, friend. A great mother's or father's day gift, Valentine's day, birthday, get well and so on. Use stamped images to illustrate or just for design.

➡ For example, "This coupon is worth one breakfast in bed".

Easter Eggs

You can use your stamps on eggs to make Easter eggs (or any other reason to decorate eggs). Hard-boiled eggs are fine for temporary use.

To make an ornament that will last, you will need to blow the egg out:

- Wash the egg.
- Poke a hole in each end of the egg very carefully. A darning needle works well for this.
- Blow the contents of the egg into a bowl.
- Rinse the inside of the egg by running water through the holes.
- Then let sit upright to dry for 24 hours.

Use very small stamps on the eggs being careful not to smear the ink.

☞ You may have to roll the egg slightly under the stamp to get the whole image on the egg.

Set the egg aside and let it dry for a few hours. When it is colored and dry, brush a urethane finish on the egg.

Now you can glue beads over the holes and put a wire through to hang the egg.

Envelopes

Use your envelopes as part of your creativity.

- Stamp envelopes to highlight the designs inside.
- Stamp confetti or streamers on a birthday card or invitation.
- Use your stamps to stamp out a cute envelope on a store bought card too.

Make your envelopes as exciting as your cards and correspondence. The mail carrier will love you!

- Another unusual envelope you can make is one made out of glossy, high-style magazine pages—like Architectural Digest, Town & Country, Photography, etc. The fun of this envelope is matching a magazine page with your card theme.

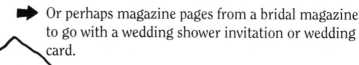

- Use a floral to go with a stamped flower design on the card.

- Or perhaps magazine pages from a bridal magazine to go with a wedding shower invitation or wedding card.

Make a template for yourself following the dimensions of the
envelope shown, or, using it as a guide, make the envelope
the size you need for the card you're making.

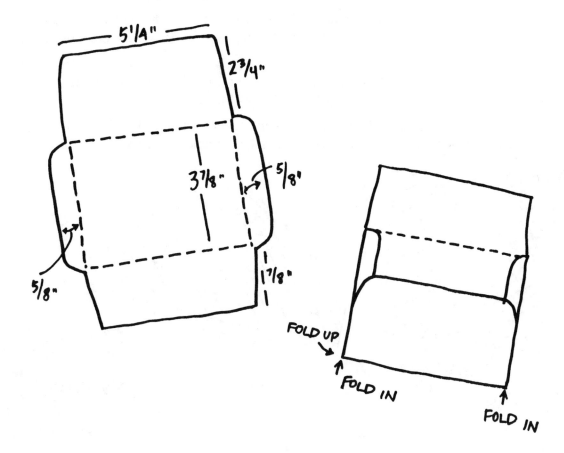

- Cut out your template.

- Put the template on the back of the page you are using. Cut out the shape from the magazine page.

☞ Arrange the template on the page so that when folded, the front will have the main design centered (or perhaps off-centered)

- Fold the envelope on the fold lines and use the glue stick to hold it together.

- Use a plain white sticker label to write the mailing address, and perhaps stamp a small design or border on the label.

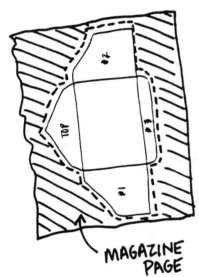

MAGAZINE PAGE

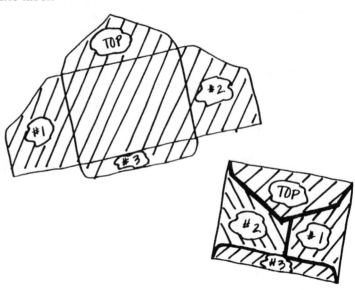

Use the templates shown as a guide for making your own to fit the envelope you are using.

Envelope Liners

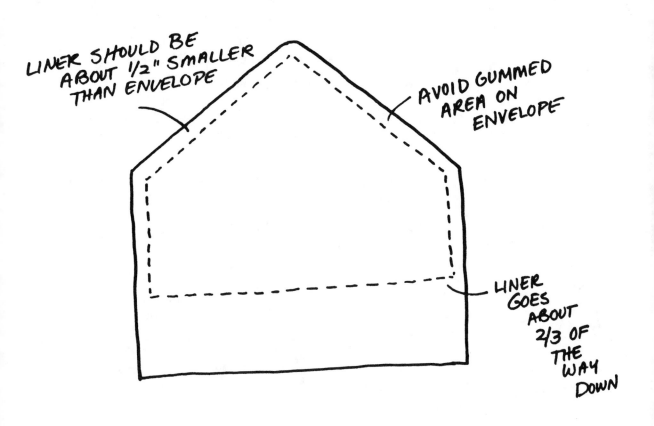

LINER SHOULD BE ABOUT 1/2" SMALLER THAN ENVELOPE

AVOID GUMMED AREA ON ENVELOPE

LINER GOES ABOUT 2/3 OF THE WAY DOWN

- Make a pattern.

- Place the pattern on the wrong side of the paper that you are using for the liner.

- Draw around the shape with a pencil, and cut out.

- Using a glue stick, glue around the top 2 edges as indicated and stick to the inside of the envelope.

- Enclose your card and fold flap.

☞ The liner should not cover the entire length of the envelope—this will keep the liner from wrinkling when you enclose your card.

☞ Gluing only the top edges of the liner allows the liner to slide as the envelope is opened or closed.

☞ Use lightweight paper, such as pretty gift wrap, or foil origami paper.

You can use your stamps to stamp on fabric as well as paper. For fabric stamping, choose bold, simple designs and deeply-etched stamps.

For embossing:

☞ Pigment-based ink, such as Color Box* work the best.

- Wash and dry the fabric.

- If possible, stretch the fabric on a stiff piece of cardboard to hold it.

- Ink the stamp well with a tapping motion on the pigment pad, and re-ink well each time you use the design.

☞ You should test on scrap material; however, un-embossed images will wash out.

- When working with the ink, you have about five minutes in which the ink stays wet enough to emboss.

- Sprinkle embossing powder on the freshly stamped image.

- Turn upside down and shake off excess embossing powder, using a sharp tapping to remove the powder from the fabric in unstamped areas.

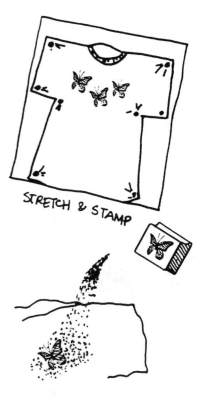

STRETCH & STAMP

EMBOSSING POWDER

Fabric Stamping

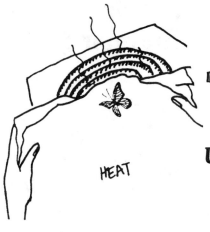

HEAT

- Heat from underneath the embossing with any heat source, <u>being careful with flammable materials;</u> or heat from above with a heat gun.

☞ Images stamped with pigment ink and embossed are permanent, however avoid hot irons and dryers when cleaning the garment

Using Fabric Ink:

- With blank foam stamp pad, pour fabric ink on the pad, working it into the foam.

- Stamp your design with the fabric ink, then clean your stamp immediately with your stamp cleaner.

- You can color in with fabric markers. Some markers you will need to heat set, others you won't. Check the instructions for the pen.

☼ Stamped t-shirts, totebags, dolls, soft albums, belts, fabric jewelry, quilts, mobiles, pillows, wall hangings are just some ideas to use for your new fabric art.

Use your rubber stamps to design flyers. Use these for business, sales, special promotions. Make an unusual birth announcement in the form of a flyer. Make unique invitations as a flyer, using rubber stamps as designs.

Flyers

- Add punch and pizazz to your gift-giving with customized gift wrap.

Gift Wrap

☞ Stamp out paper or tissue or bags to wrap.

☞ Stamp designs on flat, tightly woven ribbon for decorating gifts (or hair ribbons, etc.). If the ink bleeds and blurs the image, spray the ribbon with a clear acrylic spray first. Colorbox™ inkpads work wonderfully on ribbon. Use it just stamped, or stamp and emboss ribbons with Colorbox™.

☞ Make matching gift tags or cards. Use bookmarks as a gift tag. The bookmark makes a great gift tag with its hole on top for the tassel. While even the most beautifully decorated gift tag will eventually be thrown out, or at least put in a drawer, the bookmark can be used daily.

💡 Match stamp designs with themes such as a birthday, shower, etc. Match the gift wrap with the gift itself, such as a musical paper to go with a CD or cassette.

To make gift wrapping, it is important to use good quality paper, preferably white, glossy paper.

☞ You can use your stamps, pads, Marvy Markers™, glitter and embossing.

☞ Keep a bottle of "white-out" handy to cover any major mistakes.

☞ When thinking of a design, go bold. The larger the package, the larger the stamps should be or at least cluster stamps in groups. This way you can cover a larger area faster.

● Start with one or two images.

- Repeat them in an interesting pattern, along a diagonal, or randomly spaced.

- Group images together to make smaller images appear bigger and make a dramatic statement.

- Use Stampa Barbara's StampinGuides for an all-over pattern

● Leave plenty of "white space," you do not need to stamp over the entire paper.

- Plan out where the paper is going to be on the package first.

- Lay the paper over the gift and lightly crease along the folds.

- Now look at where the design will make the most impact.

🔅 Perhaps just stamp along the sides and top of the package; maybe concentrate the images on the top and trail down the sides in a light sprinkling of the design.

Now that you've got your design stamped and colored, go on to glitz it up, for real drama.

➡ Sparkle flowers, twinkle stars, light up the candles on a birthday wrap.

● You can either glitter the paper and then wrap the package, or wrap the package before glittering.

● Allow a few hours to let the glitter dry.

☞ Because glitter tends to spread, remember that a little goes a long way.

Another technique to use on your gift wrap is embossing.

☞ To save time, ink and spread embossing powder on a few images at a time. Then emboss them together.

☞ A heat gun works really well for this project, although a hot plate or any other heating element is fine.

🔅 Try embossing random images rather than trying to emboss the whole thing.

🔅 Look at the way the paper will be when wrapped, and emboss some of the more prominent designs.

● Embossing will give your gift wrap a very sophisticated look.

☞ Techniques for wrapping your package to give the wrap a smooth look:

- Instead of putting the seam down the middle of the gift as you normally would, arrange the wrap so the seam runs along the edge.

- Use double-stick tape under the paper to hold together, rather than invisible tape on top.

Stamp tote bags for wrapping gifts.

● You can use brown kraft bags and matte white bags.

● The white, glossy bags are great.

   🚫 **WARNING:** Test these bags, as some have a slick coat and the stamp ink will not adhere. For these bags, use stickers on the bag.

● On bags, you have more of an opportunity to make a scene or theme statement. You can actually make a giant birthday or holiday card on the front of the tote.

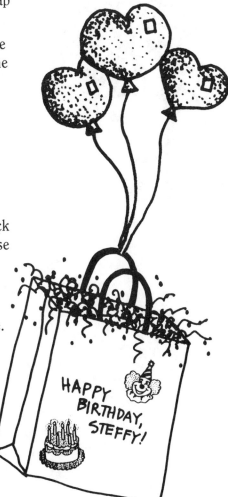

Don't forget tissue paper!

- Stamp one or two designs in a formal pattern, or just on the top corners on tissue you're stuffing into a tote bag.

☞ I like to use double tissue when I'm stuffing a tote. It adds fullness to the bag. Stamp the top sheet only.

- You can also stamp the tissue you fold over clothing in a gift box. Carry out the theme of the wrap for a coordinated look.

Use glossy white stickers, as well, in decorating packages.

- Stamp the designs on sticker paper, clustering designs for effect.

- Then color the images and glitter.

- Cut the design out, leaving a small border of white.

- Put stickers on bright-colored glossy paper for a dynamite look.

☞ <u>About mistakes</u>—most mistakes can be fixed in one creative way or another.

- Keep "white-out" handy to cover smudges and extra marks.

- Put some glitter over a questionable mark, or stamp a few little hearts or stars around, putting some over a mistake you need to cover up.

- If nothing else will work, make the design on a sticker and place it over the boo-boo.

Add color-coordinated ribbons and bows, matching gift tags, colored tissue and you've got a very impressive gift package.

Greeting Cards

Probably the first thing you think of when you think of using rubber stamps is greeting cards. That's because they are so well suited for this. The list of holidays and types of cards are endless, and you can make up your own special occasions too.

☞ Don't categorize your stamps as my "valentine stamps" or "birthday stamps". Rubber stamps are very versatile and by combining different stamps together you can get completely new looks with your stamps every time you use them.

- Use heart stamps on a Valentine for a spouse or sweetheart, combined for friendship cards, anniversary cards. Stamp a bunch of hearts and draw in strings to tie together for balloons.

- Or take the balloons you think of as your birthday stamp, color them red and green, stamp a "Merry Christmas" and your "birthday stamp" becomes a lot more versatile.

☞ Use the techniques of masking, 3-D, pop-up cards and so on to create different looks with your stamps for all different card occasions.

☞ Don't forget the technique of using marking pens to color on the rubber of the stamp rather than using a stamp pad. In this way you can use just parts of your stamp.

➡ For example, color just a teddy bear on a teddy bear stamp bearing balloons and "happy birthday"; omit "Happy Valentine's Day" on a stamp that also has a design you can use for other things.

The list of reasons for sending greeting cards are endless.

- There are the basic holidays such as Christmas and Valentine's Day, thank you's, baby, wedding and shower cards, graduation, weddings, anniversaries.

- Ground Hog's Day, first day of spring, last day of winter

- Happy New Year, Jewish New Year, Chinese New Year

- Equinox (spring or fall), over-the-hill, baby's first tooth

- First job, retirement, bon voyage

- Mother's Day, Father's Day, Grandparent's Day, April Fool's Day, May Day, Dog Days

- Thanksgiving, Thank You Very Much, Thank Goodness It's Friday

- I Love You, thinking of you, I miss you, best wishes, get well, congratulations

Invitations

Many of the same occasions that you send greeting cards may also be an occasion to make invitations. Using rubber stamps can give you many ways to make creative, unique invitations. You send an invitation to "excite, not merely invite".

● Different techniques will give you different looks. A simple, sophisticated look can be created by embossing a "You're Invited" stamp in gold or silver in the middle of a flat card. Use white, cream or even a dark colored paper for a beautiful look.

● You can use flat single sheet paper with the design and all the party information on one side. Postcards make wonderful, fun invitations.

● Use folded note cards with the design on the front and the party info inside along with some design to carry out the theme.

● Experiment with paper types to get a look you like.

   ● The glossy paper will give a very crisp, professional look, comes in many sizes, and can be embossed.

   ● Other papers may give a softer look, colors may come out in light, pastel tones.

   ● For embossing on colored papers try the different combinations of colored paper and colored embossing powders.

● Use the 3-D effect for an unusual look.

   Consider stamping confetti or fireworks over the whole front of an invitation, then stamping "It's A Party!", or "Celebrate", etc. on another sheet of paper, cutting around it and sticking it on top of the confetti with mounting tape. Perfect for birthdays, New Years, Fourth of July, etc.

   A baby shower invitation could have a bear asleep in the moon with 3-D lambs jumping over, and a cluster of opalescent stars overhead.

● Pop-up cards or pop out cards are another fun invitation look. These are great for kids parties and adult parties too.

🔆 Put your stamped design on front. For example, balloons, confetti and "happy birthday". Inside you can have a cake pop out, or more balloons, designed around the party information.

🔆 How about a Christmas open house invitation, with a large, decorated Christmas tree popping out inside.

🔆 Halloween conjures up tons of wonderful, spooky things popping out of the card!

● Die-cuts and layering make wonderful invitations.

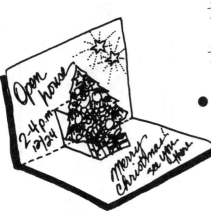

Jewelry

You can use your rubber stamps to make jewelry. Rubber stamp designs lend themselves perfectly to making paper jewelry.

Use bright colors and heavy paper.

- The glossy paper works well for this, especially if you stamp the designs on two separate sheets of paper and glue them together.

- Try embossing the designs.

- Experiment with varnishing your piece with a coat of clear acrylic spray.

- Color in and glitter up the designs.

☞ Make earrings and pins by getting findings and ear posts at hobby shops. Punch a hole in your design and make drop earrings.

☞ A 1/8" hole punch is perfect for this.

☞ Decorative buttons are fun items to make. The 1/8" hole punch works best for punching button holes.

Another technique is to use shrink plastic (as in shrink art). You can find the shrink plastic in craft stores.

- Stamp your design on plastic you have sanded.

- Use permanent ink for this (but not oil-based ink as it will ruin your rubber).

- Color in the designs with colored pencils.

    ☞ Keep in mind that the colors will get darker as the plastic shrinks.

- Cut out the designs as is, or draw a circle, triangle, square, etc. around the design first, and then cut it out.

- Use a punch to put a hole in for earrings or a jump ring.

- Then follow the manufacturer's instructions for baking, add the findings or posts—and now you have jewelry you made.

💡 You can also make buttons using the shrink plastic. This is a wonderful way to get some really unusual buttons to put on sweaters, blouses, dresses, children's clothes.

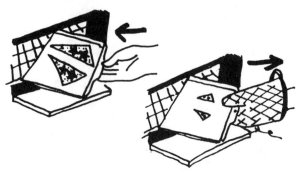

A third technique is using a clay that can be fired in your oven at home. One kind of clay is by Sculpey* and can be found at most hobby and craft stores. The clay and the stamps can be combined in many different ways.

- Knead the clay a few times.
- Roll it out like pie dough.

    ☞Use a brayer* or a rolling pin.

    ☞Put between sheets of waxed paper or plastic wrap for ease in rolling.

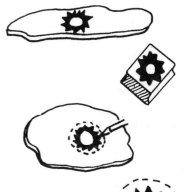

- Take a stamp design and ink it. Permanent ink works best, but you can use regular stamp ink.

    - Press gently but firmly on the clay.

    - Make sure you make an **impression** into the clay.

- You can color in with Marvy Markers at this point if you wish.

- Use an X-Acto knife and cut around the stamped image.

- Lift the clay gently with a spatula onto an old cookie sheet.

- Bake, following the directions on the package.

- You can paint the design with acrylic or enamel paint after baking.

☞Attach a pinback to the clay. Or make two designs, cut a hole in the top of each before baking, for earrings.

BACK

FRONT

- Use your imagination for making more items using this medium:

➡ magnets

➡ buttons

➡ hanging ornaments

➡ barrettes

In the kitchen

Recipe Cards:

Make personalized recipe cards for yourself and for friends as a thoughtful gift.

- Use flower or vegetable borders, or hearts, or any design that pleases you.

- Personalize recipes on recipe cards with stamp designs.

- Let your imagination and a sense of humor guide you.

  ☀ Holiday designs for holiday recipes, cows stamped on beef recipes.

  ☀ How about a little mouse on a cheeseball recipe.

  ☀ A moose on a recipe card for chocolate mousse.

Jam Jar Labels:

Decorate the labels for your canned fruits and jams with stamps. Make each one different, or come up with a distinctive design that represents "you"—your trademark. It makes your special gift that much more special.

Wine Labels:

Do the same thing on wine labels for your homemade wine. To make a sophisticated statement, try embossing your design on the label.

Labels

Use stamp designs on peel-and-stick labels for organizing all around the house.

- Label your boxes, cassettes, folders, files, slides, collections, spices and plastic containers in the kitchen, as well as labels on boxes and holders in the home office, garage, tool room, laundry room.

- Make labels with stamped designs of what is stored in the box for kids' rooms so that even young ones will recognize what goes where.

Again, it's fun to have a sense of humor with this!

Lunch
bags

Decorate lunch bags with stamps. Use the regular brown kraft paper bags and decorate with stamps to send kids to school with more than just a bag lunch! You can also buy lunch bags in white, and colors.

- Use the same stamp or a variety of stamps over the whole bag, or make a fun scene on the front half.

- Vary with the season, the holiday.

☞ Use decorated lunch bags for more than just lunches.

- Decorated bags make wonderful gift wrap for smaller presents. Put the gift in the decorated bag. Fold the top down, then punch two holes on top. Take a ribbon, pull through the holes from back to front, and tie the bow in front.

- Add a matching gift tag, punch a hole and string the ribbon through the tag before tying.

- Make decorated lunch bags as grab bags for favors for child's parties.

- Use them to hold prizes at showers, and little favors for adults' parties too.

Magnets

You can make magnets in the same way as jewelry.

- Use heavy gloss or non-gloss paper, stamp, emboss, color, glitter.

- Cut out the design and glue a small flexible magnet on the back. You can get these magnets in small squares or on a roll, and you can cut them to the size you need. Most craft stores carry these.

💡 Stamp your designs and use your alphabet set to personalize with a name, or cute saying.

💡 Use a template of a square, rectangle, or circle to surround the design and saying before cutting, if you wish.

💡 Stamp a frame. Cut the inside, and back it with a photo. Put a separate sheet on the back, and attach a magnet.

Mail Art

COMPLIMENTS BO ZARTS

All over the world there is a growing group of mail artists. They use rubber stamps either by themselves, or with other mediums to make unusual postcards, envelopes, letters, packages—anything that can go through the mail. They mail these to each other. There are more and more exhibits of mail art in museums, galleries, and rubber stamp stores all the time.

Perhaps the best, most succinct, definition of mail art was written by Russell Bloch, a mail artist known world-wide:

"Mail art, for those of you who are unfamiliar with the concept, is a process of communication whereby people exchange whatever it is that they send to each other through the mail. One thing that mail art is is difficult to define or categorize: mail art is many things. Part of the charm of mail art is that it assumes so many forms. But the underlying motive is communication.

"Widely circulated forms of mail art include letters, postcards, collage, newspaper clippings, poems, copier ("Xerox") art, found items, objects, Monopoly money, recycled (and frequently altered) junk mail, etc. Rubber stamps are used a lot in mail art, both alone as the sole medium (soul medium?) and mixed with other media (stickers, cut-out magazine pictures and words, collage, etc.) What is sent under the guise of being mail art is limited only by the imagination of the players."

COMPLIMENTS RUSSELL BLOCH

FILL THIS IN...

FROM THE BAG LADY

This is a fun and stimulating way to use your stamps and creativity. You can try this by mailing postcards to your stamping friends and asking that they mail you something in return.

You can take a large postcard, stamp a design on it. Put it in an envelope and send it to a friend. Ask that he/she stamp a design on it and send it to another friend who will do the same. Set it up so that eventually it will come back to you. My friend "The Bag Lady" in Minneapolis has a unique idea for getting unusual cards back. She stamps a large, empty bathtub on a stamped self-addressed postcard. She then mails the postcard in an envelope to friends with the request that they fill the tub and return the card to her. She has also been responsible for some wonderful mail art shows including one called the "Empty Envelope."

Try this. You will get great things in the mail, learn new ideas, and "meet" some interesting people. Check the mail call lists in both RUBBERSTAMPMADNESS (408 SW Monroe #210, Corvallis, OR 97330) and NATIONAL STAMPAGRAPHIC (1952 Everett Street, N. Valley Stream, NY 11580) to get started.

Mat Boards

Take commercial mat boards to frame your pictures and emboss designs as a border or edging. This will add a unique and personal touch to your mats, and they will look custom done (as, of course, they are).

Mat boards are too thick for the conventional manner of embossing from underneath. Since they are too heavy for fast heat penetration, follow the steps of embossing up to the point of holding them over heat. For mat boards, hold them face down over your heat source. Check about every 8-10 seconds until all the embossing powder has melted and you have your embossed design.

☞ A heat gun works really well with this type of project.

💡 Besides just embossing, try cut-outs on the boards.

- Stamp the design you've embossed on the mat board, or on a separate sheet of paper.

- Emboss this design or designs, then cut out and place on the mat board.

- Perhaps place the design half on the mat board and half off the board toward the open, picture edge.

Name Tags

When you need name tags, decorate large plain stickers with rubber stamp designs. No more of this "Hello, my name is...". By using your stamp designs you can personalize the look of the name tag, and give it some pizzazz. These designs can be used for personal use, parties, family reunions, class reunions, and business affairs.

☞ Use plain stickers you can purchase at any office supply store.

☞ Or get crack and peel label sheets from print supply stores or from your local printer.

💡 If you use the crack-and-peel sheets you can cut the labels any size you want.

💡 Cut them into shapes—such as a wreath or bell for Christmas parties, a company logo, and so on.

☞ Some stamp companies sell packaged glossy stickers under their own label.

Be creative.

- Use the name tags to carry out the theme of your party, perhaps using the same design on the label as on the invitations and decorations.

- Use 3-D and die-cuts on the labels.

- Add ribbons or streamers.

- Use glitter and glitz.

- Sprinkle colored stars or iridescent hearts on the labels with the glitter glue.

- Use small photos with the stamps.
    - ☀ Put the picture of the birthday boy or girl (child or adult!) on each name tag with a confetti design.
    - ☀ Get a yearbook photo of returning alumni on a tag with school books, or a teddy cheerleader for a class reunion.

Newsletters

Add some spice to newsletters. Using rubber stamp designs can inspire some unusual and unique ones.

- Make office newsletters, personal newsletters, Christmas newsletters.

- Make birthday invitations in the form of a newsletter.

- Salespeople, stores and companies can update their customers with the newest information in a newsletter, using stamps to decorate and accent.

Stamp the images in <u>black</u> and add the text around them. Or vice versa, add the stamp designs to the completed newsletter. If you do the text first, keep in mind the space of the stamp designs you want to add. Then reproduce your newsletter.

💡 Try colored paper in the copier!

Notepads

Take plain pads and stamp them out to make telephone pads, message pads, daily "to do" lists, grocery lists. This is great for yourself around the house, and they also make fun and personal gifts.

💡 Making notepads with personalized name stamps makes great note paper for yourself or as a gift.

☞ Most print shops will pad up these notes for a small fee.

In The Office

Rubber stamps have been around the office since the late 1800's. You associate bureaucracy with the term "rubber stamp". And rubber stamps were first made for the office— "paid", "overdue", etc. Now with all the decorative rubber stamps, office memos get a new look. Use them on routing slips and "please call" slips. Stamp bills, checks and invoices. Make name tags. Spice up your business cards. Use stamp designs to accent newsletters and flyers.

Paper

Use your imagination and experiment with different papers: glossy, vellum, scratch paper, note pads, computer paper, tissue paper, brown paper bags. Try astrobrite* papers in all different colors. By using various papers and colors, you will get some unusual and fun looks.

Don't forget you can combine the textures and colors by using 3-D, die-cuts, layering and more.

A fun change in your stamping, and a new look for your stamps, is to stamp with light inks on dark paper. You can get a very dramatic look. Try stars, clouds, snowflakes, fish— the sky is the limit. Here are some ideas for getting the look:

- Use metallic inks.

  - Pigment-based inks, such as ColorBox* work well, especially gold and silver.

  - Be sure to clean your stamps as soon as you use these inks, because they can be hard to clean later, and may clog the rubber.

  ☞ If you have a hard time getting into the small spaces of the design to get the ink out, use an old toothbrush.

- Use embossing powders.

  - Here again, the gold and silver are wonderful.

  - Use white, light colors and sparkle.

  - For a sophisticated look try a black-on-black look with a clear stamp ink and either clear or sparkle embossing powder.

Stamping light on dark can give you some spectacular results. A great look for those spooky Halloween cards, invitations, and decorations.

Another source of unusual papers for stamping is through A Class Act Papers.* They have Astrobrite* and Kromecoat* papers. You can also get many different die-cut cards, and other wonderful papers.

Parties

Design a party from beginning to end using your rubber stamps, from the invitations to the thank you notes. Create a theme and carry it through—for children's parties, dinners, showers, graduation, luncheons, office parties.

With the theme and the look you want in mind, design your invitations. This is the "introduction" to your party. Don't forget, you can also decorate the envelope with a teaser of what's inside (for example, balloons, confetti, flowers).

Now that you have the basis for the party design, you can:

- Make <u>place cards</u> and <u>name tags</u> that go with the invitation.

- Decorate <u>party hats</u>.

- Use the designs to make <u>party favors</u> and <u>party bags</u>. Make party bags out of white or colored lunch bags found in grocery stores and discount stores.

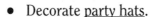

<u>Centerpieces</u> can be made with the use of your rubber stamp designs.

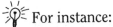 For instance:

- Take white glossy tote bags and decorate them with the stamp images.

- Color them and glitz them up.

- Then take tissue paper and again stamp a design over and over.

- Stick the tissue in the bag along with streamers and curled ribbon spilling out.

- Sprinkle around with confetti or opalescent hearts and stars.

☞ You may need to weight the bags down with something a little heavy to keep the bags from tipping.

☞ Put a plastic plant liner in the bottom of the bag and use fresh flowers, or a dried flower arrangement.

- Attach balloons to handle tote bags.

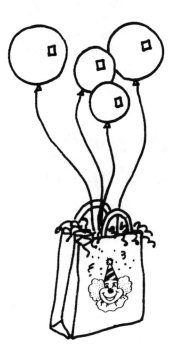

Make your own <u>partyware</u>.

- Decorate Styrofoam or paper cups.

- Make a border around paper or plastic-coated plates.

🚫 **WARNING:** Do not use plastic plates, as the ink will not dry.

- Design the paper napkins and the paper tablecloths.

💡 Make the partyware for family Thanksgiving dinner, Christmas, Easter dinner.

💡 For those occasions where thank you cards are needed, design matching ones! (This is a thoughtful gift to give the honored guest at a shower).

Personal Stationery

Design your own, unique letterheads and notecards for yourself and for gifts. Build on a theme, such as a beautiful rose in the corner, or confetti as a border all around. Then add the design to your matching envelopes.

Another wonderful way to make personalized stationery is with the use of name stamps. NameBrand Rubber Stamp Company* makes hundreds of names in different styles of writing and printing. Not only is there almost any name, spelled any way, but you can special order names and addresses.

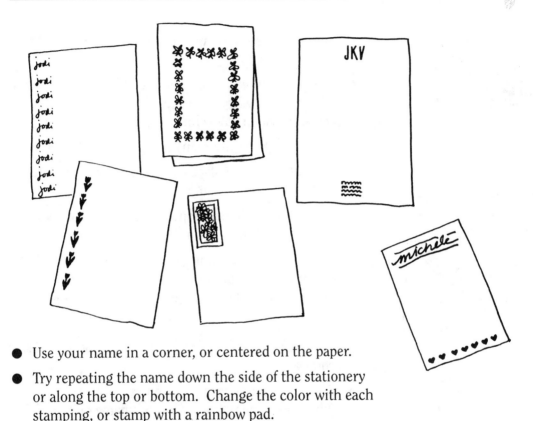

- Use your name in a corner, or centered on the paper.

- Try repeating the name down the side of the stationery or along the top or bottom. Change the color with each stamping, or stamp with a rainbow pad.

- Emboss the name, using gold or silver for a formal note, a silvery sparkle over rainbow colors for a fun look.

- There are also some very impressive ways to make unusual stationery.

- Stamp the name (or any image you want) on a scrap of glossy paper

- You can emboss, or just stamp in a color, color it and glitter as you wish. Now cut around the name or design leaving some white space.

- From here there are many things that can be done.

- Use a glue stick to place the name on colored note paper.

- Put double-stick foam tape on the back of the design and attach to your note paper.

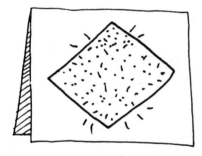

For some truly eye-catching stationery, use colored foil with your design. I prefer metallic origami foil paper, but other colored paper will give equally interesting effects.

- Cut the foil in strips, or squares, or any other fun shape you want.

- Glue the foil to your notecard first with the glue stick. Then glue the cut out name on top of the foil.

- Try putting the name on straight with the foil, or at an angle, staying within the foil space, or overlapping onto the notepaper.

Photo Albums And Scrapbooks

Use rubber stamps to add some fun and interest to your photo albums and scrapbooks.

- Take your rubber stamps and make borders and frames around pictures or articles.

- Make scenes to introduce a subject—for example, use balloons, confetti, "happy birthday" before and around pictures from a birthday party.

- Let a sense of humor surround happy memories.

- A talk balloon with words can be added to a picture of someone who looks like they're talking; or a thought balloon with outrageous thoughts added to a very serious-looking person.

🚫 **WARNING:** If you're using stamps in a photo album where the pictures are not protected by plastic, do not let the stamped images rub on the photos. You could put pictures and designs on only one side of each album page to be really careful.

Photo Greeting Cards

Make your own photo greeting cards.

You need:

- ✔ large-size glossy folded notecards
- ✔ glue stick
- ✔ stamps, pads
- ✔ photos

💡 You can put the photo on the front of the card and the greeting inside, or stamp out a holiday scene on the front and put the photo on the inside.

💡 Try putting a picture inside a die-cut card with a heart or star cut-out on the front. Arrange the photo so you see the faces through the heart or star! This makes a wonderful valentine's card!

- Take the stamps you have chosen and stamp a border all around the picture.

- Color the border and glitter it if you wish.

- There are wonderful stamps of hearts, holly, "ho ho", balloons, small flowers. How about stamping "paws" around your animal's picture or a family photo with your pet in it.

- Snowflakes and stars and clouds are all good stamps for backgrounds.

- Use glue on the back of the photo to tack it down inside the border.

In the same way we made photo cards, we can make picture frames using the same large size, glossy cards.

Picture Frames

- Use tracing paper to make a pattern around your picture so you know how much you want to show through.

- Use this pattern to cut out the front of the card.

- Center the photo on the inside.

- Use the glue stick to tack down the picture. Then use the it again to tack down the four sides of the back to the front.

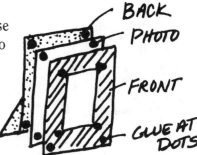

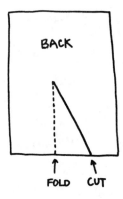

FOLD   CUT

To make an <u>easel back</u>:

● Follow the pattern below cut from the back sheet—cut this first before gluing down the picture.

● Or add an extra piece on the back for an easel.

☞ You can also glue a magnet strip on the back for a magnetic frame.

On the front make a great border for your photo. And don't forget, you can use your alphabet and number sets and name stamps sets to personalize the frame.

Placecards

When making your party, don't forget placecards. For a sit-down dinner, or a luncheon, shower, etc. design your own placecards around the theme of your party. You can make the cards very simple, or very elaborate.

● Stamp a design, color it and glitter it for an easy, unique, but simple card.

● Go all out. Make die-cut place cards with a design cut out at the top.

● Make use of the 3-D technique, and let a bunch of balloons float over the name.

Whatever the party theme, custom-designed placecards will add a special touch to your party.

Postcards

Use your rubber stamps to make wonderful postcards that even the mailman will enjoy!

- Make a scene on one side of the card, and a message and address on the other side.

- Incorporate the stamp design along with the words as well, working the address into the design.

☞ Creative Impressions* makes a pad of postcards specifically for stamping. One side is glossy for the design, the other a matte finish for correspondence.

There is a whole art of rubber stamping called Mail Art (See MAIL ART). Postcards or envelopes are designed with rubber stamp images and sent through the mail. There are Mail Art gallery shows and correspondents mainly concerned with mail art. This is an exciting, growing art form.

Puzzles

Make your own puzzles.

Stamp out a scene, a message, a note, an invitation, a card, etc. on heavy cardboard—then cut to make a jigsaw. Mail the pieces for a new twist in greeting cards and invitations! This makes a wonderful learning tool for kids, and a fun way for them to make their own party invitations.

☞ You can buy blank jigsaw cards to stamp.

Turn letters into rebus puzzles using stamp images in place of words. You can get rebus stamp sets made just for this purpose. There is just as much fun in the making of it, as it is in getting a letter like this.

Ribbons

Tightly woven ribbons, such as satin, can be stamped with rubber stamps. Colorbox™ pigment ink stamp pads are perfect for stamping on this fabric.

- Use a solid stamp pad, or rainbow pads with a design that does not need to be colored in.

- You can just stamp the design, or you can emboss the image.

   ☞ If you stamped with a rainbow pad, use a transparent embossing powder, such as clear, pearl, sparkle, rainbow sparkle, silvery sparkle. (See FABRIC STAMPING for more on embossing on fabric).

- For a design image that you want colored in, emboss first, then color it with fabric markers. The embossing keeps the colors from bleeding into each other.

○ **WARNING**: Since the Colorbox™ inks are not permanent if not embossed, do not use these unembossed on items you will be washing.

- Use small stamps for ribbon. Great for birthday gifts,

  wedding gifts (try embossing the design in gold or silver), Christmas and other holidays.

- Use your name stamps for personalized ribbons on all your packages.

- Use word stamps, such as "thank you," "happy birthday," "Merry Christmas."

- Carry out a theme with matching ribbon for gifts wrapped with your custom designed gift wrap.

- Use them for girls' hair ribbons.

Rubber Stamp Party

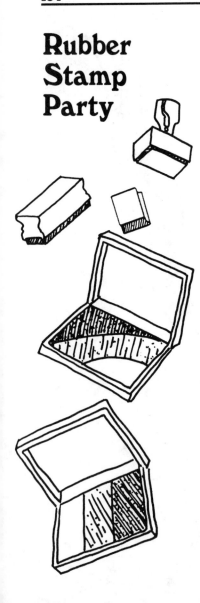

Give a rubber stamp party for children or adults!

For children:

A rubber stamp party is a great way to keep kids busy and productive. Depending on the children and your patience, the age of seven is a good age to start (although, there have been many successful parties for five year olds). Lay out stamps, pads, pens. Sit down with them and explain the uses of rubber stamps and what they can do with them. <u>Most importantly, teach them how to clean the stamps when they finish using each one, and give them each damp paper towels to clean the stamps.</u> Then give them a project and watch great imagination at work. Some good projects:

- party hats
- visors
- little bags
- bookmarks
- a notebook to stamp a story

You could read or tell a story, and have stamps relating to it. (See CHILDREN'S PARTIES for more information.)

For adults:

Organize a group get-together for a specific purpose—such as to make holiday cards, valentines, etc. or just to stamp and exchange ideas.

💡 Have everyone bring some of their own stamps and ideas for maximum possibilities.

- It is amazing to watch others use your stamps in ways you hadn't thought of.

- This can break some of your preconceived notions of what your stamps are to be used for.

- By using each other's stamps, you will find some new and exciting ones you didn't know about.

💡 Have a stamp exchange.

- Swap stamps you don't like with other's cast-offs.

- This is a great way to get new stamps and get rid of ones that are just taking up space. One person's trash is another's treasure!

From these group get-togethers you can form a stamp club that meets once a month, or so. As a group you can attend rubber stamp workshops or classes.

Stickers

Make your own stickers. This is another fun project for kids. Many rubber stamp companies carry plain white stickers. Or you can get Crack-n-Peel sticker paper at most printers or paper supply houses. Use the stickers to decorate packages and bags, make scenes with a multiple of sticker images. Make a set of Bookplates for a gift using a sheet of sticker paper. Use stickers as a teaching tool too.

Use glossy sticker paper to design beautiful gift wrap.

- Make a design on the sticker paper, color and glitter it.

- Cut out the design leaving a border of white space, and stick this on bright-colored paper or tote bag.

- Make one large scene, or a border of decorative images, each cut out of the sticker paper and stuck at even intervals or randomly on the package.

① MAKE SOME →
STICKERS +
CUT THEM OUT

② →
PUT
STICKERS
ON PACKAGE

Use sticker paper to make a 3-dimensional butterfly to put on a greeting card, or on package wrap.

☞ The butterfly stamp you use must have a symmetrical design. (This can be done with other symmetrical designs as well).

- Stamp out three butterflies on a sticker.
- Color the designs.
- Leaving the backing on the sticker paper, cut out all 3 butterflies.
- Fold each butterfly in half vertically, stamped sides together.
- Take the paper backing off one of the butterflies, and stick a small section on the back of your hand

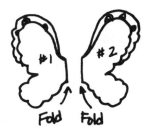

- Remove the backing off another butterfly. Now you have 2 butterflies with the backing off.

- Place the sticky right vertical half of first butterfly to the sticky left vertical half of the second butterfly. You now have half a side of each butterfly stuck together, and half of each with the sticky side together.

- Remove the paper backing from the third butterfly.

- Place the sticky left vertical side of the third side to the sticky right side of the second butterfly matching outside edges.

- You now have two sticky halves remaining (half of #1 and half of #2)

- Trim any uneven outside edges.

- Place both sticky sides of the butterfly on your card, letter, package, etc. When you stick down the two sides be sure they are stuck as close as possible to each other.

You can stamp faces, arms, hands with your rubber stamps. This can work like face painting. Stamp the design, and then you can color in the image. This is also a good way to stamp a hand for a carnival or dance re-entrant.

Tattoos

🚫 **WARNING:** Be sure to use **water-based** stamp pads, and **water-based** pens.

Rubber stamps make wonderful gifts for teachers. There are many "teacher's stamps" to pick from. A stamp, or set, and a small rainbow ink pad makes a great gift for teacher.

Teacher's Gifts

💡 Buy a stamp that says "A note from teacher", or "Just a note", for example.

- Get a box of 10–12 glossy, folded notecards, and stamp the design on each card.

- Color the design, and glitter it.

- You can even decorate each envelope.

- Wrap the notecards and envelopes together with a ribbon.

☞ If your children are young and there will be quite a few teachers to gift, keep the stamp for yourself and next year you will have new teachers to give to!

🔅 Let your child make a personalized calendar for the teacher.

- Stamp in all the special school events, the school holidays.

- Make sure your child stamps in his/her own birthday on the calendar!

- Stamp any other special events, or make little notes.

- The top of each page can be stamped with an appropriate scene for the month, or big school event, or just something special to stamp.

Teachers And Other Care Givers

There are a variety of "teacher's" stamps out there. Ones that say "good work", "terrific", "star reader", "please sign and return" and so on. When we think of teachers using rubber stamps, grading papers comes to mind immediately. This alone is a great reason to use rubber stamps in the classroom. Children look forward to getting a stamp of praise on their work, and using rubber stamps are more cost-effective than putting disposable stickers on every paper!

☞ Rubber stamps can be stamped with rainbow stamp pads to get color, without coloring all the graded papers.

☞ Use stamps as a method of grading—the more a design is repeated, the better the work.

☞ Use stamps that tie in with the theme or topic being worked on.

☞ The ideas for grading papers can be very creative and educational at the same time.

Using rubber stamps for grading papers is basic, but there is so much more they can be used for:

☞ Make flash cards for math, game boards to learn skills.

☞ Have students stamp out stories and write their story to go along with the sequence of their stamps.

☞ Make progress charts for the students.

　　💡 For example, a chart for reading can be lots of fun to keep up, letting the students stamp a square for each book they read.

　　💡 Because stamp images are pre-verbal, a progress chart in nursery school or day care will also work really well for young children as well.

☞ Illustrate a class or school newsletter with rubber stamp images.

☞ Create banners and room decorations for different holidays.

☞ Giving the class a project and stamps to work with is a wonderful way to teach basic composition and balance. They learn how to make borders, use a focal point, and background designs. It can also teach cooperation and socialization. Let them create a classroom calendar, recipe cards, greeting cards, wrapping paper.

☞ Use rubber stamps to make games.

- Bingo is a wonderful game for using image, number and/or letter recognition. Rule out bingo boards on plain paper. Stamp the images on the boards and on pieces of colored construction paper.

- Make maze games, letting a student stamp a star, heart, animal paw along a path to connect two images.

- For the more advanced students, let them make chess sets.

☞ Set stamps out and let the kids make A to Z books, using stamp images.

☞ Make maps with stamped legends, teaching social studies and history with the stamps.

☞ Make weather maps, too, using images to show snow, wind, sun, high and low pressure.

☞ Give the students small stamps they can use to repeat and make designs of geometric shapes.

☞ When students are allowed to use the stamps, <u>begin with some basic rules</u>. Teach them how to clean their stamps, and ask that stamps be cleaned after each use. Spend the last 5 minutes of stamping by putting the stamps back in some order.

And above all, have fun!

Decorate tennis shoes following the steps for fabric stamping. Add "jewels", use puffy fabric paint to decorate with, fluorescent fabric paint and glitter paint.

Tennis Shoes

Tranquilizers

Rubber stamps help stamp out stress. Just sitting down to your basket of stamps and working with them will reduce your blood pressure. Often I take my stamps out for one project and end up stamping for hours. Rubber stamping can be mesmerizing. And it seems the more you stamp, the more your creative juices will flow. One idea seems to lead to another. And, while you're stamping, your problems end up on the back burner. It is as if you are stamping all your cares away!

Many therapists use rubber stamps when working with physically or mentally handicapped patients. The simplicity of the stamps makes them very appropriate for physically and mentally ill people. Using them requires little energy or manual dexterity. And you get instant gratification with them. You stamp and you get an image. Stamps are a good way to <u>express</u> feelings before one is willing to talk about them.

Rubber stamps bring out the inner child in all of us. Perhaps that's one reason stamping has become so universally popular. Just sitting down to stamp will bring out the creativity we didn't even know we had. We needn't be inhibited when using rubber stamps, since it doesn't matter that you "can't draw a straight line." And there is no right or wrong way. In fact, the "wrong" way is often how new and exciting ideas come about.

Traveling

Rubber stamping is a wonderful, portable hobby. For those who travel often, for business or for rest and relaxation, rubber stamps can be a wonderful way to wind down at the end of the day. It is also comforting to have personal things with you that can keep you busy on your off hours.

- You can stamp practical items, like "Wish You Were Here" postcards, fun letters, unusual business correspondence.

- Or you can just experiment with your stamps, as this could be considered "down" time anyway.

- ☞ You can have a small travel case filled with the stamps and accessories you want to travel with. These could remained packed in their own case, ready to go at any time.

Valentine's Mailboxes

Wrap a shoebox that has a mailbox slot cut out at the top.

- Use glossy paper that you have decorated by stamping hearts, flowers, I Love You, etc.

- Color and glitz it up.

- ☞ See the section on GIFT WRAP for specific instructions on planning where to stamp and how to wrap.

- Consider adding small cut up doilies, and pasting on stamped, cut-out hearts to complement the designs.

- Try doing some stamped hearts with double-stick mounting tape for a 3-D effect.

Window Cards

TAPE

ACETATE

These cards are not that hard to make, and the effect is magnificent. You can get the look of scenery outside a window, I Love You and hearts inside a heart, a snow scene in a crystal snow ball, and more.

For this project you will need:

✔ glossy, folded card the size you will need for your stamped images

✔ a piece of glossy paper the same size as the front of your card

✔ an X-Acto knife

✔ #.003 or #.005 clear acetate sheet

✔ regular double-stick tape

✔ foam-backed double-stick tape (optional)

➡ Let's make a snow scene in a crystal snow ball as an example:

● Stamp the crystal ball on your card.

● Stamp in the other designs on the front of the card, such as "Happy Holidays" and the snow flakes.

● Use your X-Acto knife to cut out the see-through crystal.

● Take the extra piece of glossy paper that is the same size as the front of the card and stamp your scene.

☞ To make sure it is lined up inside the ball, place this sheet under the opening where it is going to go. You can either mark where the opening will be with a light pencil, or carefully stamp with the paper positioned under the front.

☞ The Stamp Positioner™ works well for this.

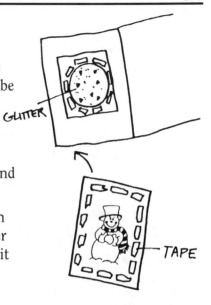

GLITTER

- Open the folded card and place double-stick tape around the back of the ball opening.

- Cut a piece of the clear acetate at least 1/2" larger than the opening in the card all the way around. Lay it over the opening, sticking it down on the tape. Make sure it extends over the opening.

TAPE

- Put double-stick tape around the edges of the scene on the other paper with the scene stamped and colored on it.

- Put double-stick tape again around the edges of the cut opening over the acetate.

- If you want more space, put foam-backed tape on the card between the tape layers. This is optional, but it allows the glitter and confetti to float around.

- Before sticking the two layers together, sprinkle glitter or opalescent confetti inside.

I see you
will have a
happy holiday
... with snow!

🔆 You can use this same technique to make a window with an outside scene with the glitter confetti. Cut a large window in a postcard size glossy card, back it with a beach or snow scene, and make a "Wish You Were Here" card.

🔆 Take a die-cut heart card, put "I Love You" showing through the heart window with opalescent heart glitters.

🔆 Make a crystal ball and use a cut-out photo of someone inside with an "I see you will…" card as a birthday or congratulations card.

I see you will be falling in love...

➡️ "I see you will have a very happy year. Happy Birthday."

➡️ "I see you will be president of the company someday. Congratulations on your promotion."

🔆 You can also use two sheets of acetate, instead of using a plain piece of glossy paper behind the acetate layer. This will let a design inside the card show through.

This card is so much fun I am sure you will think of many other ways to use this technique.

WISH YOU WERE HERE! ♥abby

Stamping on wood gives a more permanent surface for your rubber stamping. Look around at all the bare wood in craft stores, frame stores, even furniture stores that could benefit from your creative hand and a few rubber stamp designs.

Wood Objects

- Pigment inks such as Color Box™ can be used with rubber stamps to stamp images on wood.

  - Using the pigment ink and embossing powder works beautifully.

  - If you emboss, use an oven or a toaster oven at 300°, or a craft heat gun.

  ☞ Heat guns are perfect for embossing on wood, paper and fabric.

- Fabric ink can also be used to stamp on wood, and does not need to be embossed.

🚫 **WARNING:** Fabric ink is not a water-based ink, so cleaning your stamps with alcohol must be done quickly, or the ink will dry and clog your stamps.

☞ Raw wood tends to bleed, and some finished wood is too slick to hold the ink.

- You will get the best results by first finely sanding the wood smooth.

- Then finish with a polyurethane stain, or wipe a latex paint into the wood.

- If you want a natural unstained, unpainted look, seal the wood before stamping with olive oil or tung oil.

- I have used a clear acrylic spray to seal raw wood.

Experiment stamping in bright colors such as dark blue, purple, black, silver, gold. After stamping you can paint it in if you wish. Try adding colored stones and other findings after you've finished stamping.

Mini-Shaker boxes carried at most craft stores come in lots of sizes and make ideal stamped items. Stamp on picture frames and even furniture. Craft stores are wonderful places to find many unfinished wood pieces that would look great stamped.

The Beginning

This is not the end, but merely the beginning of hours of fun and creativity for you and your stamps.

GLOSSARY

Astrobrite paper: Bright-colored, heavy stock paper.

Brayer: A craft tool which looks like a small rubber rolling pin on a handle. Often used with linoleum block printing.

Brush markers: **Water-based** marking pens with a long, broad tip for coloring in stamp images, or coloring directly on the marker.

ColorBox™: Pigment-based stamp pads. The ink is very wet, so it is excellent for embossing, or stamping on vellum paper.

Dazzle™ Glue: Hero Arts Rubber Stamp Company's brand of glitter glue.

Double-Stick foam-backed tape: Mounting tape which is sticky on both sides of a foam strip. Comes packaged in squares or on a roll.

Easter grass: Green cellophane shred that looks like grass.

Embossing: The technique of using a combination of stamps, ink and embossing powder to achieve a raised, stamped image on paper.

Embossing ink: Very wet, thick, clear ink to be used on a blank stamp pad, and used with stamps and embossing powder.

Embossing powder: When sprinkled on wet ink stamped on paper, and then heated, the powder melts and gives a raised look to designs.

Fabric paint: Paints made specifically for stamping on fabrics that will be permanent after stamped.

First generation stamping: The first impression made with the stamp after inking.

Foil origami paper: Metallic foil paper, cut in squares and packaged specifically for use in the art of Origami (Japanese folding art).

Glue Stick: As used in this book, a glue stick made by Zig. It comes in a pen-type applicator. The glue itself is dry and tacky.

Heat gun: A heating element that looks like a hair dryer, but gets extremely hot without blowing. Available in craft and hobby stores.

Kromecoat™ paper: A brand of cover-weight, glossy paper, double-coated on one side of the paper. This glossy paper works well for stamping and gives a crisp look to stamp images.

Mail Art: Stamped, or otherwise hand-designed, postcards and envelopes made as communication to be mailed. See the section **Mail Art.**

Overstamping: To stamp another stamp either wholly or in part over another image or process (such as a "wash" in the water-color technique).

Prisma™ glitter: A fine or medium-fine loose glitter that comes in iridescent and colors. It has no adherent, so it is to be sprinkled over glue from a glue stick or glitter glue.

Rainbow stamp pads: Pads for stamps that generally have 3 or more colors on the same pad. Some rainbow pads come with one pad rainbow colored, others have separate strips side by side.

Second and third- generation stamping: After the first stamping, succeeding stampings made without reinking the stamp. To regain moisture with each impression, "huff" on the stamp.

Sparkles: Any type of glittery add-ons sprinkled on glitter glue or glue stick, such as opalescent stars, hearts, snowflakes, mylar in all different shapes.

Stamp pads: Felt or foam pads with **water-based** ink for use with rubber stamps.

Wash: Using a wet watercolor brush to extend the colors of a stamped image.

Word stamps: Stamp designs that have sayings on them, such as "Happy Birthday", "Best Wishes". To be used alone or in combination with other stamp designs.

X-Acto knife: A craft knife with a razor blade as the cutting surface. For the purposes in this book, a #11 blade works best.

RESOURCES

A STAMP IN THE HAND
Carson, CA

ALL NIGHT MEDIA
San Rafael, CA

ARTWORKS, INC.
Jackson, MS

DENAMI RUBBER STAMPS
Seattle, WA

HERO ARTS RUBBER STAMPS
Berkeley, CA

PERSONAL STAMP EXCHANGE
Petaluma, CA

POSH IMPRESSIONS
Brea, CA

RAINDROPS ON ROSES
Raleigh, NC

RUBBERSTAMPS OF AMERICA
Saxtons River, VT

MARVY MARKERS
Marvy/Uchida Corporation

PRISMA GLITTER
Gick Publishing Company

ZIP 2-WAY GLUE
Distributed through:
E & K Success

acetate sheets - 176,177,178
add-ons - 33,34,35,37,98-99
baby gift - 108
baby wipes - 12
barrettes - 140
bingo - 172
borders - 53,56
boxes - 105-107, 180
brayer - 139
brush markers - 7,20,21,23-
   25,40,82,86
burner - 39
buttons - 138, 140
calendar - 99-100, 107-109,
   170, 172
centerpieces - 152
colored foil - 156
correspondence
   correspondence - 116
   Mail Art - 144-146
   personalized stationery -
     154-156
   postcards - 145, 161, 175
double-stick foam tape -
   69,156,176,177
E-Z Store* - 14
easel back - 160
Easter grass - 99
eggs - 117
Elfa* basket system - 14
emboss
   embossing - 39-43,123,128-
     129,137,156,179
   embossing ink - 43
   embossing powder -
     39,41,42,123,151

fabric stamping
   fabric - 53,123,124,173
   fabric ink - 124,173,179
   ribbons - 126,162-163
   tennis shoes - 173
family history calendar - 109
flash cards - 171
flip books - 104
games - 172
gift wrap - 53,125-127
grading - 171
heat - 39
heat gun - 39,146,179
heating element - - 39,42
hot plate - 39
maze games - 172
name tags - 147-148,152
National Stampographic* - 146
origami paper - 156
party
   children's parties - 111-
     113,164
   invitations - 53,134
   parties - 111-113,152-
     154,164-165
   party bags - 152
   party favors - 152
   party hats - 152
   partyware - 154
   placecards - 152,160
   rubber stamp party - 164-165
personalizing - 154-156
photos - 77,148,158,160
progress charts - 171
ribbon - 126,162-163

RubberStampMadness* - 146
Sculpey * - 139
See-Thru Paper™ - 57,58,59
shrink plastic - 138
Stamp Positioner™ - 56-59,177
Stampa Barbara* - 53,56
StampinGuides™ - 53-55,127
stickers - 130,141,147,166-168
teachers - 169-173
toaster - 39,179
tote bags - 152,153
X-Acto knife -
   63,64,100,139,176

Notes: